QUIET MOMENTS
WITH PADRE PIO

QUIET MOMENTS
WITH PADRE PIO

120 DAILY READINGS

COMPILED BY PATRICIA TREECE

CHARIS

SERVANT PUBLICATIONS
ANN ARBOR, MICHIGAN

Charis Books is an imprint of Servant Publications especially designed to serve Roman Catholics.

Published by Servant Publications
P.O. Box 8617
Ann Arbor, Michigan 48107

Cover design: Left Coast Design, Portland, Oregon
Photographs: Courtesy of The National Center for Padre Pio, U.S.A., and Our Lady of Grace
Capuchin Friary, Italy. Used by permission.

03   04   05   06   07   10   9   8   7

Printed in the United States of America
ISBN 0-56955-129-4

LIBRARY OF CONGRESS CATALOGING-IN-PUBLICATION DATA

Pio, padre, 1887-1968.
    Quiet moments with Padre Pio / compiled by Patricia Treece.
        p.   cm.
    Includes bibliographical references.
    ISBN 1-56955-129-4 (alk. paper)
    1. Spiritual life—Catholic Church.   2. Pio, padre, 1887-1968—Correspondence.
3. Capuchins— Italy—Correspondence.   4. Catholic Church—Italy—Clergy—Correspondence.
I. Treece, Patricia.   II. Title.
BX2350.2.P55   1999
271'.3602—dc21   99-12790
                                                        CIP

This book is for B. Smith,
Beloved cousin, companion, and faithful friend
Because you love Padre Pio

and

For Blessed Pio's spiritual son
Father Joseph Pius Martin, O.F.M. Cap.
of Our Lady of Grace Friary
San Giovanni Rotondo,
in gratitude
for your many years of help
in my writings on Padre Pio

ACKNOWLEDGMENTS

My thanks to Bert Ghezzi for letting me immerse myself in a second saint for this series and to my editor, Heidi Hess, for not only excellent editing but for her patience and kindness as I struggled to master both a new computer and new software during the project. For all kinds of spiritual and mentoring support with my computer during this period my loving gratitude to Francis and Mary Levy. For research assistance my warm appreciation to sisters Julia C. Ciccarone and Maria Calandra of the National Centre for Padre Pio, Inc. in Barto, Pennsylvania, and to Barnabite Father Anthony Bianco of Allentown, Pennsylvania. Finally, as always in anything I do involving Padre Pio, my heartfelt gratitude to Father Joseph Pius Martin, O.F.M. Cap. of Our Lady of Grace Friary in San Giovanni Rotondo, Italy, to whom I have dedicated this book. May the Lord reward you all!

A NOTE ON HIS LETTERS

Due to his poor health early in his priesthood, as well as due to the distances involved, before fame constricted this apostolate, Padre Pio gave spiritual direction by letter to a large number of people. Revealing that he both knew the hearts of men and women and the Christian scriptures by heart, these letters deal with every human problem, from worries over money, health, and relationships to legal troubles as grist for the mill that leads souls to God. Although he makes it plain that he loves many of those whom he addresses, it is also clear that, as an editor put it, "the sole motive Pio has for writing" is "the sanctification of the [recipient's] soul" and his or her "progress to union with God through charity."

Editor's note: While we have been careful not to change the meaning of Padre Pio's words, in some cases passages were condensed or otherwise adapted in the interest of space or clarity. In most cases ellipses were not used, except when the passage was a first-person account of one of Padre Pio's mystical experiences that may not otherwise be widely available in English at this time.

INTRODUCTION

Imagine a twentieth-century living crucifix, a man with wounds like those of Christ in his side, his hands, and his feet. Can such a medieval, otherworldly, or neurotic individual—to consider possible labels for one with the wounds called the stigmata—possibly have anything to say to you and me?

I didn't think so years ago when I first heard of Padre Pio, the stigmatized Capuchin Franciscan monk of San Giovanni Rotondo in southern Italy. Those dark, piercing eyes under bushy brows scared me, as did the whole idea of a spiritual warrior called by Christ himself (in a series of youthful visions) to engage in lifelong conflict with Satan. This was a man, then, like Pio's spiritual hero St. Paul, who would suffer with Christ to redeem sinners both by call and by choice (see Col 1:24). Grim and forbidding this twentieth-century Paul seemed to me. Certainly no one with whom I'd want to spend quiet moments.

Yet I was looking at Padre Pio in those days through my own fear: fear of my sinfulness and God's wrath and fear that suffering might thrust its ugly face into my life. Above all I feared Padre Pio's insight that love for God, like human love, may be measured by one's willingness to suffer for the beloved. Love that wants only "goodies" from God is not love at all.

Today I see that, yes, Padre Pio for fifty years had real wounds that hurt and bled, wounds that, as he pungently put it to a gawker, were not "decorations." Yet if they were painful, these wounds were also, he said, a mystical fountain of life for the man who bore them, as well as for the thousands who shared in the fruits of his willing crucifixion and constant prayer. Ask me today about Padre Pio and I will speak of reparatory suffering that God does not need but sometimes permits certain valiant souls as a grace-filled participation in Christ's work.

I will also describe an earthy man with a big laugh, a man who loved jokes and pranks, a man not born with an easy temperament, who all his life fought tendencies to irritability and the brusque reply.

It was this real person, not some plaster saint, who wanted to join in Christ's redemption of the world, understanding that there was a price to pay to wrest souls from darkness. "When I know that a person is afflicted, what would I not do to have the Lord relieve him of his sufferings! Willingly would I take upon myself all his afflictions in order to see him saved," Pio said and meant it, his heart burning with compassionate love for humanity. That love for others, of course, was the overflow, the spillage, of the love pouring into the saint from God, love so great he feared to burst trying to "contain it in the narrow cell of my heart."

Yet paradoxicallly, this ecstatic who lived with a foot and a half in the supernatural dimension—a man whose bilocations, odor of sanctity, visions, gift of reading hearts, and charism of healing I've described from first-person testimonies in other books as well as in this one—remained so down to earth that the Italian man of letters who arrived at Padre Pio's friary in San Giovanni Rotondo looking for the "haloed saint" found the real Padre Pio the very last person he would have suspected. (See reading #14.) Why? Because the real Padre Pio was so natural, so—in the best sense of the word—*ordinary.*

A consummate spiritual advisor to people living as teachers, as housewives, as doctors, and as construction workers, as well as to priests and seminarians, was this gifted soul who knew the Scriptures and the writings of many saints forward and back. His words of wise advice to these many friends—whom both he and they considered to be the saint's "spiritual children"—are words of life for us all. In fact, as we come to know this man who could be so shy, tender, and gentle, as well as cranky and exhausted like you and me, we come face to face with the mystery of God. In God and his saint, some will be surprised to find not wrath but mercy, not icy judgment but warm, tender compassion. May these quiet moments with Padre Pio soak you, dear reader, in both these attributes of the Holy of Holies.

1 ⤦ DON'T WORRY ABOUT TOMORROW

—July 4, 1917 letter to Capuchin seminarians

I recommend to you to have a firm and general proposal to always serve God with all your heart; do not worry about tomorrow. Think about doing good today. And when tomorrow comes, it will be today and then you can think about it. Trust in Providence. It is necessary to make provisions of Manna for only one day and no more. Remember the people of Israel in the desert.

2 ⊸ ON THE MIXED MOTIVES OF THE HUMAN HEART

—June 18, 1917 letter to Maria Gargani, schoolteacher and later foundress of the Institute of the Apostles of the Sacred Heart

You told me about the frivolity and inconstancy of your heart, of being continually tossed about by the winds of its passions, and as a consequence, always staggering. [I believe you.] But I also believe no less firmly that the grace of Jesus and the resolution you made are continually in your heart, where the flag of the cross is always hoisted, and where faith, hope, and charity pronounce courageously: Long live Jesus!

I agree, my beloved daughter, that the inclinations of pride, vanity, self-love, etc. are mixed up in almost all your actions, but I do not agree that, for this reason, they become the true motives of your actions. One day tormented by the above-mentioned inclinations while he was preaching, St. Bernard said, "I haven't begun for you [pride, vanity, etc.], nor do I want to finish for you."

Do the same when you are assailed by these [passions] and live tranquilly because Jesus is with you always and you rest sweetly on his heart. [The good deeds you do] do not have a lesser value even when they are done in a weak, heavy, and almost-forced manner.

3 ⊷ PRAYER

Prayer is the oxygen
of the soul!

4 ❧ To Grow in Love

—April 20, 1915 letter to noblewoman Raffaelina Cerase

I beg you in our most tender Jesus not to yield to this fear of not loving God. I understand very well that nobody can worthily love God, but when a person does all he can himself and trusts in the divine mercy, why should Jesus reject one who is seeking him like this?

Say to Jesus, as St. Augustine invariably said: "'Give what you command and command what you will.' Do you want great love from me, Jesus? I too desire this, just as a deer longs to reach a flowing stream, but as you see I have no more love to give! Give me some more and I'll offer it to you!" Do not doubt that Jesus who is so good will accept your offer.

5 ❧ To Love God Is to Be Certain of Possessing Him

—October 23, 1914 letter to Raffaelina Cerase

The [instinctive] movement of our hearts is a movement towards God, which is nothing more than loving our own true good.

Joy is born of happiness at possessing what we love. Now, from the moment at which the soul knows God, it is naturally led to love him.

By loving God the soul is certain of possessing him. When a person loves money, honors, and good health, unfortunately, he does not always possess what he loves, whereas he who loves God possesses him at once.

This idea is not the product of my own mind but is found in Holy Scripture where we read: *He who abides in love abides in God and God abides in him.*[1]

---

1. John 15:10

6 ✧ Advice on Loving God

—May 19, 1914 letter to Raffaelina Cerase

You are trying to measure, understand, feel, and touch the love which you have for God. But, my dear sister, you must accept as certain that the more a soul loves God, the less it feels this love.

I am not able to explain this truth very clearly, but you can take it as certain that the matter is as I have said. God is incomprehensible and inaccessible; hence the more a soul penetrates into the love of this Supreme Good, the more the sentiment of love towards him, which is beyond the soul's knowledge, seems to diminish, until the poor soul considers that it no longer loves him at all.

In certain instances it seems to the soul that this is really the case but that continual fear, that holy circumspection which makes one look carefully where to place one's feet so as not to stumble, that courage in facing the assaults of the enemy, that resignation to God's will in all life's adversities, that ardent desire to see God's kingdom established in one's own heart and in the hearts of others are the clearest proof of the soul's love [for God].

7 ❧ ALWAYS GROW IN CHARITY

—March 30, 1915 letter to Raffaelina Cerase

Grow always in Christian charity. Never tire of advancing in this queen of all the virtues. Consider that you can never grow too much in this. Love it very much. Let it be more than the apple of your eye, for it is truly most dear to our divine Master. In an altogether divine phrase, he calls it "my precept."[1] Oh, yes, let us greatly esteem this precept of the divine Master and all difficulties will be overcome.

The virtue of love is exceedingly beautiful and to enkindle it in our hearts the Son of God was pleased to come down himself from the bosom of the Eternal Father, to become like us in order to teach us and make it easy for us, with the means he left us, to acquire this most eminent virtue.

Let us ask Jesus insistently to give us this virtue and let us make greater and greater efforts to grow in it. Let us ask this, I repeat, at all times.

---

1. John 15:12

8 ⋄ The Desire to Love God Is the Love of God

—December 14, 1916 letter to schoolteacher Erminia Gargani[1] (sister of Maria Gargani)

You become sad at the love you feel for God. It seems to you that it is little more than nothing. But, my good daughter, don't you yourself feel this love in your soul? What is that doubt, or rather, what is that ardent desire that you yourself express to me? Well, you should know, my dear daughter, that *in divino* the desire to love is love.

Who placed this yearning to love the Lord in your heart? Don't holy desires come from above? Are we perhaps capable of arousing in ourselves one single desire of that kind without the grace of God which sweetly works within us? If there was nothing but the desire to love God in a soul, everything is present already; God himself is there, because God is not, nor can he be, anywhere except where there is a desire for his love.

Rest assured as regards the existence of divine love in your heart. And if this desire of yours is not satisfied; if it seems to you that you always desire without possessing perfect love, all this signifies that you must never say "enough!"; we cannot and must not stop on the path of divine love.

---

1. Erminia entered a convent, but when her parents strenuously objected, she followed Padre Pio's advice and returned home to live out her life as a consecrated laywoman.

9 ❧ A Desire Never Completely Satisfied on Earth

—March 30, 1915 letter to Raffaelina Cerase

For pity's sake, my Raffaelina, don't think me more than I am. It seems to me that I have no charity at all. In the many years I have spent at Jesus' school all the desires I have for the good God have not yet been satisfied. I feel within me all the time something I cannot define, something akin to a void. I would like my love to be more perfect and no matter how much I strive to do this, I continue to feel ever more intensely this desire to love. I understand only too well that this desire can never be completely satisfied as long as we are wayfarers on this earth and this is where all my sufferings [of unrequited longing] start.

10 ❧ THE SUREST TEST OF LOVE

—Three letters to Raffaelina Cerase, dated July 14, 1914; May 15, 1915; and June 8, 1915

Don't be daunted by the cross. The surest test of love consists in suffering for the loved one. If God suffered so much for love, the pain we suffer for him becomes as lovable as love itself. In the troubles which the Lord bestows on you, be patient and conform yourself gladly to the divine Heart in the knowledge that all is a continual game on the part of your Lover.

The more you are afflicted the more you ought to rejoice, because in the fire of tribulation the soul will become pure gold, worthy to shine in the heavenly palace.

*

Don't be disheartened if … nature cries out for comfort. Jesus' human nature also asked that the chalice might be taken away.

*

[Human nature] naturally wants to escape [suffering], for man was created to enjoy happiness. As long as we remain in this world we shall always feel a natural aversion for suffering.

Be quite sure that if in the apex of our spirit, we submit to it for love of God, [our humanity's natural aversion] becomes a cause of merit for us if we hold it in check and subdue it.

11 ❧ The Crown Is Won in Combat

—May 19, 1918 letter to teacher Maria Anna Campanile, one of ten children from a family close to Padre Pio

The storm that is raging around you is a sure sign of love. This is not just a personal conviction of mine, but an argument from Scripture which tells us that temptations are proof of the soul's union with God: *My son, when you are about to serve God, prepare yourself for temptations.*[1] It is an indication of God's presence deep down in the soul. "I will be with him in trouble," says the Lord.[2] Therefore the apostle St. James exhorts souls to rejoice when they see themselves tormented by various calamities and numerous contradictions: *Count it all joy, my brethren, when you meet various trials.*[3]

The reason is that the crown is won in combat. If we realize that every victory we obtain has a corresponding degree of eternal glory, how can we fail to rejoice, my dearest daughter, when we find ourselves obliged to face many trials in the course of our life?

May this thought console you, my daughter, and may you be encouraged by the example of Jesus *who in every respect has been tempted as we are, yet without sinning.*[4]

---

1. Sirach 2:1   2. Psalm 91:15   3. James 1:2   4. Hebrews 4:15

12 ❧ HAVE COMPLETE TRUST IN GOD

—July 28, 1914 and May 15, 1915 letters to Raffaelina Cerase

Let us consider Jesus' love for us and his concern for our well-being and then let us be at peace. Let us not doubt that he will invariably assist us with more than fatherly care....

The more numerous your enemies become, the more you ought to abandon yourself with complete trust in the Lord. He will always sustain you with his powerful arm so that you may not stumble.

Before the Lord abandons us, we should have to abandon him. In a word, we should first have to close the door of our heart to him and even then, how many times does he not stretch out his hand to us to arrest our headlong dash towards the precipice! How many times, when we had abandoned him, has he not readmitted us to his loving embrace!

How good our God is! Blessed forever be his hand which many times alleviates our sufferings and marvelously heals our incurable wounds.

* * *

Without divine grace, could you have been victorious in all the crises and all the spiritual battles which you have had to face? Well, then, open your soul more and more to divine hope, have more trust in the divine mercy which is the only refuge of the soul exposed to a stormy sea.

13 ❦ A Visit to Pietrelcina

—Padre Pio's spiritual son, Giampaolo Mattei, visits Pietrelcina (pop. 3,000), where Padre Pio was born and raised

Mystery is in the air here.... [Everything] reminds one that Christianity is not made up of the things that please one, but of what pleases a God, who has made full use of mystery.

... A visit to the so-called Torretta (the little tower) can be disquieting. It is a little room that clings to a rock. Even with the help of the iron railing it is not easy to climb to the top. Padre Pio lived here as a student. There is a little table and a bed. Poverty prevails, the same poverty that one encounters a few meters further on ... at number 32 of Vico Storto Valle ... [where] one encounters the dust and sweat from the street and stable.... Here on May 25, 1887, Padre Pio was born.... These rooms render homage to his peasant father who more than once had to emigrate to America [to earn the money for Pio's studies preparing him to enter the seminary] and to his mother who said to her son when he left home to become a priest: "Don't worry about my tears, follow your vocation and may the Lord make you a saint."

14 ❧ Not What He Expected

An eminent man of letters who arrived at Padre Pio's friary, [believed that] certain "saints" look "holy," [with] … eyes turned to Heaven, foreheads illuminated by a ray of light, arms stretched out or crossed on their chests….

Among the praying friars he searched for a Padre Pio like that.

"Do you see him?" his friend whispered.

"I think so," he replied. But he was wrong. Padre Pio, he later admitted, "was the one I would have described as the least mystical."

The visitor's second surprise came next morning as Padre Pio said mass, at times almost "making a face," shutting his reddened eyelids.

"He must be very cold," the observer thought. But afterwards his friend said, "Did you see he was crying?"

The visitor reflected these were not the "beautiful showy, shining tears" befitting his idea of a saint but the tears of a man who must weep but resists.

Finally, in the confessional, he found only "the usual country priest."

The real Padre Pio, he summed up, was "a friar with no ascetical poses, a priest with no mystical attitudes; yet one whose authenticity and originality are beyond dispute, the sincerity of his soul and the power of his spirit above all suspicion."

15 ❧ "THE INDOMITABLE SPIRIT OF A WARRIOR"

Journalist Giambattista Angioletti went to San Giovanni expecting to see "a little friar." Instead he said when Padre Pio approached he appeared as "an ancient warrior with a dark tunic open at the collar." Angioletti was "dumbfounded at the unexpected appearance of the man who was full of energy and vigor and who, instead of speaking of heavenly things [to him], spoke of … present-day-politics; of agricultural reform; raging against the lazy, the cowardly…."

The journalist wrote, "like lightning, I had the certainty that true faith springs from energy. Furthermore … from violence, from the indomitable spirit of a warrior. In order to tear evil from the hearts of men, two things only are adequate; first sweetness, and then strength, and this is irreplaceable…. One of these without the other can do nothing."

16 ❧ BEWARE THESE THREE

—*October 23, 1914 letter to Raffaelina Cerase*

Do we want to live a spiritual life, moved and guided by the Spirit of the Lord? Let us take care, then, to mortify our selfish spirit which puffs us up, makes us impulsive, and leads to aridity of soul. In a word, we must be careful to subdue vainglory, irascibility, and envy, three evil spirits to which most men are slaves. These three spirits are extremely opposed to the Spirit of the Lord.

17 ❧ GOD SPEAKS THROUGH SCRIPTURE AND OTHER HOLY BOOKS

—*July 14, 1914 letter to Raffaelina Cerase*

Help yourself mainly during this [troubled] period by reading holy books.[1] I earnestly desire to see you reading such books at all times, for this reading provides excellent food for the soul and conduces to great progress along the path of perfection. By no means [is it] inferior to what we obtain through prayer and holy meditation. In prayer and meditation it is we ourselves who speak to the Lord, while in holy reading it is God who speaks to us. Try to treasure these holy readings as much as you can and you will very soon be aware of a spiritual renewal within you.

Before beginning to read, raise your mind to the Lord and implore him to guide your mind himself, to speak to your heart and move your will.

---

1. By "holy books" Pio refers primarily to the Scriptures but he also includes writings of the Doctors of the Church and other saints.

18 ⊸ To Follow Jesus, One Must Think About Him

—Letters to Fra Marcellino Diconsole da Foggia,[1] Erminia Gargani, and Antonietta Vona[2]

Propose therefore to make yourself worthy of him, or rather similar to him, in the adorable perfections by now known to you from reading holy books and the Gospel. But to be able to imitate him, it is necessary to reflect and meditate constantly on his life.

*

Each day [we must think] on the life of the One we intend to take as our model. From reflection is born esteem for his acts, and from esteem springs the desire of imitation.

*

[So] assiduously study Jesus Christ and his divine doctrine and [then] follow his illustrious example, which he places before us as a model in divine Scripture.

---

1. Padre Pio wrote this seminarian on November 17, 1918; Diconsole left the Capuchins in 1921.
2. Upon this woman's death in 1949, Padre Pio said, "she lived in a hidden manner in the most profound humility and in a state of continual suffering which she bore with a serene and joyful soul, and she died like a little candle, totally consumed in God and for God."

19 ❧ THE IMPORTANCE OF READING SCRIPTURE (PART I)

—From a July 28, 1914 letter to Raffaelina Cerase

I am horrified at the damage done to souls by their failure to read holy books.

Listen to the way the holy Fathers exhort us to apply ourselves to this type of reading. St. Bernard recognizes four degrees or means by which to reach God, namely, reading and meditation, prayer and contemplation. As proof of what he says, he quotes the divine Master's own words: *Seek and you will find, knock and it will be opened to you.*[1] He says that by reading Sacred Scripture and other holy and pious books, we are seeking God; by meditation we find him, by prayer we knock at the door of his heart, and by contemplation enter the theatre of divine delights which has been opened to our mental gaze by reading, meditation, and prayer.

St. Jerome teaches St. Paulinus: Always keep the holy book in your hands that it may nourish your soul. [To a widow he recommends] reading Scripture and the writings of those Doctors [of the Church] whose doctrine is holy and wholesome. To Demetriade he writes: Love reading Holy Scripture if you want to be loved by divine wisdom.

---

1. Matthew 7:7; Luke 11:9

20 ❧ The Importance of Reading Scripture (Part II)

[Regarding] the power of holy reading, consider the conversion of St. Augustine. Who won this great man to God? Neither his mother by her tears nor the great St. Ambrose by his divine eloquence. [What violent conflicts Augustine] endured in his poor heart because of his enormous reluctance to give up his lewd sensual pleasures. But while he battled with such tumultuous feelings he heard a voice say: "take up and read." He obeyed, and as he read St. Paul['s epistle], the thick darkness in his mind was dispelled, all the hardness vanished from his heart, and from that moment he devoted himself completely to the service of God and became the great saint honored today.

St. Ignatius Loyola, as the result of spiritual reading[1] which he made with the sole desire to escape from the boredom of a painful infirmity, was transformed from a captain in the army of an earthly king into a captain at the service of the king of heaven.

St. Columban through [such] reading to please his wife found himself completely changed.

Now if [reading Scripture can] convert worldly men into spiritual [ones], how very powerful must not such reading be in leading spiritual men and women to greater perfection?

---

1. Convalescing from a wound, Ignatius was handed a book on the life of Christ and a book on the lives of the saints.

21 ❧ THE SAINT'S FAVORITE SCRIPTURE WRITER

—October 23 and November 16, 1914 letters to Raffaelina Cerase

In introducing you to the model of the true Christian, my guide will be my beloved apostle St. Paul. His sayings, all filled with heavenly wisdom, entrance me. They fill my heart with heavenly dew and take my soul out of itself. I cannot read his letters without experiencing a fragrance that spreads all through my soul, a fragrance that reaches the very apex of my spirit.

* * *

Whenever I read his letters, which I prefer to all other holy writings, words cannot express my relish for them.

22 ❧ Wait Tranquilly for Heaven's Dew

Anxiety is one of the greatest traitors that real virtue and solid devotion [to God] can ever have. It pretends to warm us to do good works, but doesn't and we grow cold; it makes us run only to make us trip. One must be careful of this on all occasions, particularly at prayer. And to better succeed it would be well to remember that graces and consolations of prayer are not waters of this earth, but of Heaven. Therefore all our efforts are not sufficient to make them fall, even though it is necessary to prepare oneself with great diligence but always humbly and tranquilly. One must keep one's heart turned toward Heaven and wait from there the heavenly dew.

23 ❧ SAFE IN THE DIVINE ARMS

—*April 23, 1918 letter to Erminia Gargani*

Do not anticipate the problems of this life with apprehension, but rather with a perfect hope that God, to whom you belong, will free you from them accordingly. He has defended you up to now. Simply hold on tightly to the hand of his divine providence and he will help you in all events, and when you are unable to walk, he will lead you.

Why should you fear when you belong to this God who strongly assured us: "We know that in everything God works for good with those who love him"?[1] Don't think about tomorrow's events, because the same Heavenly Father who takes care of you today will do the same tomorrow and forever.

Live tranquilly, [removing] from your imagination that which upsets you and often say to our Lord: *Oh God, you are my God and I will trust in you. You will assist me and be my refuge, and I will fear nothing* because not only are you with him, but you are in him and he is within you. What can a child fear in the arms of its father?

---

1. Romans 8:28

24 ❧ THE PURPOSE OF MEDITATION

Why distress yourself because you cannot meditate? Meditation is a means to rise to God, but not an end. The final purpose of meditation is the love of God and one's neighbor. Love the first with all your soul and without reservation; love the second as another self, and you will have arrived at the final purpose of meditation. [If you can't *think* about God because you are] called to contemplate God let yourself be conquered and don't desire to [think about him], which would be the first part of meditation. Apply yourself [instead] to move the heart sweetly to resolutions and affections towards God, which would be the second part of meditation and, I would almost say, the all. Use the first part of meditation when you must [to] come to the second part. But when the good God already places you in the second part, don't wish to turn back, which would be the same as spoiling everything.

25 ❧ THE SPIRIT OF GOD IS A SPIRIT OF PEACE

The Spirit of God is a spirit of peace. Even in the most serious faults he makes us feel a sorrow that is tranquil, humble, and confident and this is precisely because of his mercy.

The spirit of the devil, instead, excites, exasperates, and makes us feel, in that very sorrow, anger against ourselves, whereas we should on the contrary be charitable with ourselves first and foremost.

Therefore if any thought agitates you, this agitation never comes from God, who gives you peace, being the Spirit of Peace, but from the devil.

26 ❧ CALM IN THE STORM

—October 24, 1913 letter to Padre Agostino, one of Padre Pio's two spiritual directors at this time

How important it is to avoid being upset by the trials and troubles of this life, for these things always tend to contract the heart rather than opening it up to trust God.

27 ❧ THE WORTH OF A TRULY CHRISTIAN LIFE

—*April 11, 1914 letter to Raffaelina Cerase*

Not all of us are called by God to save souls and propagate his glory by the noble apostolate of preaching. Remember, moreover, that this is not the only means of achieving these two great ideals. One can promote God's glory and work for the salvation of souls by means of a truly Christian life, by praying without ceasing that "his kingdom come," that his name be "hallowed," that "we may not be led into temptation," and that he "deliver us from evil."

This is what you ought to do, offering yourself continually to the Lord for this purpose. You may be perfectly sure that this is the highest form of apostolate that any one can carry on, which is precisely what Jesus tells us.

28 ❧ An Ecstasy at the Friary

—In Venafro in 1911, recorded by Padre Agostino, who was present

"Oh Jesus, I recommend that person to you. Convert him, save him. Don't only convert him, because after he could lose your grace, but save him, save him. Didn't you shed your blood for him also? Jesus, do you want to go? Stay another while. It is so nice to stay with you."

29 ❧ THE FIRE OF LOVE

—March 26, 1914 letter to Padre Benedetto, Padre Pio's second spiritual director at this time

I no sooner begin to pray than my heart is filled with a fire of love. This fire does not resemble any fire on this lowly earth. It is a delicate and very gentle flame which consumes without causing any pain. It is so sweet and delightful that it satisfies and satiates my spirit to the point of insatiability. Dear God! This is a wonderful thing for me, something I will perhaps never understand until I get to heaven.

[My] desire [for God] is not extinguished by the delight experienced, but is rather perfected by this delight.

30 ❧ Why in Jesus One Cannot Remain Selfish

—May 31, 1918 letter to Maria Anna Campanile

Now you will understand, my good daughter, why the soul that has chosen divine love cannot remain selfish in the Heart of Jesus, but feels itself burn with love for its brothers and sisters.

Why does this happen? My daughter, it is not difficult to understand. Since the soul no longer lives its own life, but lives in Jesus who lives within the soul, it must feel, want, and live the same sentiments and wishes of the One who lives within it. And you know, my most beloved daughter, even if you learned of this at a late stage, of the sentiments and desires which animate the Heart of this Divine Master for God and humanity.

31 ❧ THE GRACE OF COMPASSION FOR OTHERS

—March 26, 1914 letter to Padre Benedetto

Deep down in my soul, it seems to me, God has poured out many graces of compassion for the sufferings of others, especially with regard to the poor and needy. The immense pity I experience at the sight of a poor man gives rise deep down in my soul to a most vehement desire to help him, and if I were to follow the dictates of my will, I should be driven to strip myself even of my clothing to cover him.

When I know that a person is afflicted in soul or body, what would I not do to have the Lord relieve him of his sufferings! Willingly would I take upon myself all his afflictions in order to see him saved, and I would even hand over to him the benefits of such sufferings if the Lord would allow it.

I see quite clearly that this is a most singular favor from God because in the past, although by divine mercy I never neglected helping those in need, I had little or no pity in a natural way for their sufferings.

32 → Baptism Is Not the End of Struggle

—*November 16, 1914 letter to Raffaelina Cerase*

The life [of] the Christian consists in stripping oneself of the vices of the man of this world and in clothing oneself in the virtues which Jesus Christ taught.

The Christian sanctified by baptism is not exempt from the rebellion of the senses and passions; the holy apostle [Paul] himself suffered considerable interior distress from [such] rebellion, which led him to utter the following complaint: *I of myself serve the law of God with my mind, but with my flesh I serve the law of sin,*[1] that is, the law of concupiscence.

This is to be said for the spiritual consolation of many unfortunate people who experience the sharp conflict within themselves to which a hot temper or lustful desires give rise. They do not want to feel or to harbor those impulses, that ill-feeling toward others, those vivid pictures presented by their imagination, those sensual promptings. Poor things! Quite involuntarily these feelings surge up and produce a conflict within them, so that in the act of wanting to do something right they feel violently impelled towards something wrong.

Some think they are offending God when they feel this violent

interior inclination to evil. Take heart, you chosen souls, for in this there is no sin, since the holy apostle himself, a chosen instrument, experienced this dreadful conflict within.[2] Even when carnal impulses are violently felt, there can be no sin when the will does not consent to them.

1. Romans 7:25
2. See Romans 7:16

33 ❧ A Heritage of Joy

Padre Pio's family was so devout, neighbors called them "the family for whom God is everything." But this did not mean they were dour. The trait people most recall about Padre Pio's father, Grazio Forgione, is his joyfulness. A man with a deep love of God, who would walk around an ant, saying, "why should the poor creature die?" Forgione loved to sing with gusto and communicated "a contagious joy."

Padre Pio's mother Giuseppa De Nunzio, who was equally devout, also "knew how to keep merry company." Once her little Francesco (Padre Pio's birth name) upbraided her that her remark "What good looking turnips; I'd like to eat some" as they passed a field might be a sin (in case she was thinking of simply taking one) then asked her to pick him some figs from a tree they passed. "Oh, it's a sin to eat turnips but not a sin to eat figs!" she teased.

Padre Pio's own sense of humor and his love of pranks and jokes was remarked upon by his friends. It cannot be overestimated how important this heritage of joy was to his maintenance of good mental health and freedom from morbidity in his unique apostolate as a spiritual warrior.

34 ❧ On Padre Pio's Guardian Angel

—Testimony from Fr. Eusebio, who assisted Padre Pio from 1961-65

[This guardian angel] began his work early when Padre Pio was still a boy. He took the semblance of another child and made himself visible to him. Later on, advanced in age and sanctity, Padre Pio will rightly call his guardian angel "the companion of my infancy." This name reveals an intimate relationship between the little Francesco [Padre Pio's name as a child] and his dear Angel. A companion is not a person whom we see once or rarely, but a person whom we often see and with whom we are friends. We love him, and in the case of the child Padre Pio, play games [with him] too. [This] heavenly friend gladdened his boyhood and made him long for heaven.

That's why Padre Pio had for his Angel a deep felt, most tender and confidential devotion.

35 ❧ TESTING THE MYSTIC'S AUTHENTICITY

Beginning in early 1912 when Padre Pio was living in his native Pietrelcina for health reasons, one of Padre Pio's two spiritual directors, Padre Agostino of San Marco in Lamis, decided to test the authenticity of Padre Pio's sanctity. He did this by writing to him in French and Greek, languages Padre Pio did not know. Padre Pio had no problem receiving letters even in Greek. He had his Guardian Angel translate them for him.

Authenticity for this is found in a statement appended to the end of one of these letters. Dated August 25, 1919, it is written by the parish priest Salvatore Pannullo. Pannullo writes: "I, the undersigned, testify under oath that when Padre Pio received this letter, he explained its contents to me literally. When I asked him how he could read and explain it, as he did not know even the Greek alphabet, he replied: 'You know, my Guardian Angel explained it all to me.'"

36 ⊸ CONSIDER YOUR GOOD ANGEL

—April 20, 1915 letter to Raffaelina Cerase

May your good angel be your breastplate to ward off the blows that the enemies of our salvation aim at you.

O Raffaelina, how consoling it is to know one is always under the protection of a heavenly spirit who never abandons us, not even (what an admirable thing!) when we are actually offending God! How delightful is this great truth to the one who believes! Who is to be feared, then, by the devout soul who is trying to love Jesus, when accompanied by such an illustrious warrior? Was he not, perhaps, one of the multitude who joined St. Michael up there in the heavens to defend God's honor against Satan and all the other rebellious angels, to vanquish them in the end and drive them down to hell?[1]

Let me tell you that he is still powerful. His love has not lessened and he can never fail to defend [you]. The fact that we have close to us an angelic spirit who never leaves us for an instant from the cradle to the grave, who guides and protects us like a friend or a brother, must really fill us with consolation.

---

1. See Daniel 10:13; Revelation 12:7

37 ❧ My Good Angel Prays for Me

—April 20, 1915 letter to Raffaelina Cerase

This good angel is praying for you and offers to God all your good works, your holy and worthy desires. When it seems to you that you are alone and abandoned, don't complain that you are without a friend to whom you can open your heart and confide your woes. For goodness sake, don't forget this invisible companion who is always there to listen to you, always ready to console you.

O delightful intimacy, O blessed companionship! If all men could only understand and appreciate the very great gift which God in his exceeding love has given us by appointing this heavenly spirit to guide us! Call to mind his presence very often. Thank him and pray to him. He is so considerate and sensitive. Respect him. You must always be afraid to offend the purity of his gaze.

Frequently invoke this kindhearted angel. Often repeat the beautiful prayer: "Angel of God, my guardian dear, to whom God's love commits me here, ever this day be at my side to light and guard, to rule and guide."

At the hour of death, you will behold this good angel who accompanied you during life and was so generous in his motherly care of you!

38 ❧ "DON'T YOU SEE ALL THOSE GUARDIAN ANGELS?"

—Testimony by Padre Alessio Parente, O.F.M. Cap.

Being at Padre Pio's side for almost six years, I often heard it said: "Father, as I will not be able to come to see you again, what should I do if I need your prayers?" And Padre Pio would reply: "If you cannot come to me, send me your Guardian Angel. He can take a message from you to me and I will assist you as much as I can."

One day, [as] I was sitting by his side, Padre Pio [was] fingering his rosary. There was such a peace and calm around him that I felt encouraged to ask some questions. To my surprise, [he replied]: "Come on, my son, leave me alone. Don't you see that I am very busy?"

"Strange," I thought. "He is sitting down fingering his rosary and he says he is busy." While I remained totally silent thinking it was not true that he was busy, Padre Pio turned to me and said: "Didn't you see all those Guardian Angels going backwards and forwards from my spiritual children bringing messages from them?"

I retorted: "Father, I have not seen even one Guardian Angel, but I believe you because you tell people every day to send you theirs."

39 ✧ Precious Time

Who can assure us that we will be alive tomorrow? Let us listen to the voice of our conscience, to the voice of the royal prophet: "Today, if you hear God's voice, harden not your heart."[1] Let us not put off from one moment to another [what we should do] because the [next moment] is not yet ours.

*

Oh, how precious time is! Blessed are those who know how to make good use of it. Oh, if only all could understand how precious time is, undoubtedly everyone would do his best to spend it in a praiseworthy manner!

---

1. Hebrews 3:7-8

40 ❧ THE HEART REBELS

You are distressed that your will [doesn't share] your resignation to the divine plan. Are you really sure of this statement?

Unfortunately when you utter your act of acceptance of God's will, you want to feel this in your heart also with a kind of perceptible sweetness. But have I not told you that the state of purgation in which the Lord has placed you consists precisely in stripping your soul of that delightful feeling [it used to have]?

Consider Jesus' act of acceptance in the Garden and how much it cost him, making him sweat a sweat of blood! Make this act yourself when things are going well and also when they go against you. Don't be upset and don't worry about the way in which you make your act. We know that nature shrinks from the cross when things are hard, but we cannot say the soul is not submissive to God's will when we see it carrying out that will in spite of the strong pull it feels in the opposite direction.

If your will flees from rebellion you may be certain that the will, in its own way, has uttered its act of acceptance.

41 ❧ DON'T WEARY YOURSELF

—September 19, 1914 and February 23, 1915 letters to Raffaelina Cerase

You tell me that on account of your sleepy, distracted, fickle, and most wretched soul, frequently with the addition of physical complaints, you cannot bear to remain in church for [very long]. Don't worry on this account. Make an effort to overcome vexation and boredom and don't weary your mind excessively with very long and continued prayers when your heart and mind are not so inclined.

Try, meanwhile, to withdraw during the day, when possible, and in the silence of your heart and in solitude offer your praises, your blessings, your contrite and humble heart, and your entire self to the heavenly Father.

*

Here's what you could do during the bad [weather] season and your period of convalescence. Continue to rise rather late in the morning, then go to church, receive Holy Communion, spend a short time in adoration before Jesus in the Blessed Sacrament, then return home at once. Make your thanksgiving for Communion at home.

As regards [not] hearing Mass on weekdays, don't be upset and don't torment yourself about it. Jesus knows all [the reasons it can't be done] and he will also know how to make allowances for you.

42 ❧ Wings That Lift Us to God

Humility and purity of conduct are the wings which raise us up to God and in a manner deify us. Remember this: the sinner who is ashamed to do evil is closer to God than the upright man who is ashamed to do good.

43 ❧ Self-Centeredness Is Always With Us

—February 12, 1917 letter to Maria Gargani

All that you experience as regards [your] little impulses is of no importance at all. These assaults of the passions, my dearest daughter, that take place within us without our willing it, are inevitable while we are pilgrims on earth.

It is precisely for this reason that [St. Paul] cried to heaven in the bitterness of his heart: *Alas, poor man that I am! I feel two men within me, the old and the new; two laws, the law of the senses and that of the spirit; two workings, that of nature and that of grace. Ah! Who will free me from this body of death?*[1]

My daughter, let us convince and resign ourselves before this great and terrible truth. Self-love never dies before we do. This certainly causes us to suffer but we must still be resigned and patient with ourselves, and in our patience we will possess our souls, as the divine Master tells us. This possession is all the more secure, the less it is mixed up with worries and disturbances, even where our imperfections are concerned.

---

1. Romans 7:23-24

44 ❧ Ignore Ridicule

Be always faithful to God in keeping the promises made to Him, and do not bother about the ridicule of the foolish. Know that the saints were always sneered at by the world and worldlings; they have trampled them under foot and have triumphed over the world and its maxims.

45 ❧ We Are Not Alone in Our Trials

—November 26, 1914 letter to Raffaelina Cerase

Be steadfast and firm in your faith and be on the alert, for in this way you will avoid all the evil snares of the enemy ... [according to] the warning given us by the prince of the apostles, St. Peter: *Be sober, be watchful. Your adversary the devil prowls around like a roaring lion, seeking someone to devour. Resist him, firm in your faith.* Then for our greater encouragement he adds: *Knowing that the same experience of suffering is required of your brotherhood throughout the world.*[1]

Yes, beloved daughter of Jesus, renew your faith in the truths of Christian doctrine, especially at times of conflict. And renew in a most particular way your faith in the promises of eternal life which our most sweet Jesus makes to those who fight energetically and courageously. You should be encouraged and comforted by the knowledge that we are not alone in our sufferings, for all the followers of the Nazarene scattered throughout the world suffer in the same manner and are all exposed like ourselves to the trials and tribulations of life.

---

1. 1 Peter 5:8-9

46 ❧ PARADOXICAL VICTORY IN DEFEAT

—September 7, 1915 letter to Raffaelina Cerase

When a man engages in a fight with another man, the one who is afraid, the one who is wounded, who falls to the ground and sheds his blood is considered to have lost the fight. However, in life, he who trembles before this same God against whose strength nothing is of any avail, for everything yields to his word, he, I say, who is crushed by the sight of the wounds produced by his own failings and drags himself along face downwards in the dust, who humbles himself, weeps, sighs, and prays, this man triumphs over God's justice and obliges God to show him mercy.[1]

It is impossible for God not to welcome these demonstrations of goodwill and not to give way and surrender to you. God's power triumphs over everything, but humble and suffering prayer prevails over God himself. It disarms him, vanquishes and placates him, and makes him almost a dependent and a friend.

---

1. See Esther 8:3; Genesis 32:28

47 ⟿ WEANING THE SOUL

—January 9, 1915 letter to Raffaelina Cerase and July 27, 1917 letter to Maria Gargani

[A child's] weaning causes him to suffer [but it is necessary so that, properly nourished,] he will become a fine man.

God deals with our souls in this manner. He wants to win us over to himself by having us experience abundant sweetness and consolations in all our devotions. But who does not see the great danger that surrounds this kind of love of God? It is easy for the poor soul to become attached to the [sweetness and consolations], while paying very little attention to [real] love which alone make it dear and pleasing to God.

Our most sweet Lord hastens to the rescue. When he sees that a person has acquired sufficient virtue to persevere in his holy service without the attractions and sweetness which arrive through the senses, he then [offers] that person greater holiness [by removing] the delightful feelings experienced in meditations, prayers, and other devotions.

* * *

[When this occurs] we must still be content, doing [our] duty without any compensation for the present. By doing this, our love for God is selfless. One loves and serves God in this way at one's own expense, a behavior [of mature] souls.

48 ❧ How to Receive the "Bread of Angels"

—September 7, 1915 letter to Raffaelina Cerase

Let us approach to receive the bread of angels[1] with great faith and with a great flame of love in our hearts. Let us await this most tender lover of our souls in order to be consoled in this life with the kiss of his mouth. Happy are we, Raffaelina, if we succeed in receiving from the Lord the consolation of this kiss in the present life! Then indeed will we feel our will inseparably bound at all times to Jesus' will, and nothing in the world can prevent us from willing what our divine Master wills. O my God and my glory, then alone can we say: Yes, O divine lover, O Lord of our life, *Your love is better than wine, your anointing oils are fragrant.*[2]

When our most tender Lord enables one to pronounce these words as the spouse in the Song pronounced them, one feels such a sweetness that one is well aware that Jesus is very near.

---

1. the Eucharist
2. Song of Songs 1:3

49 ✤ THE AFFABILITY OF JESUS

There are moments when I call to mind the severity of Jesus and am about to feel distressed, but then when I consider his affability, I am completely consoled. I cannot help abandoning myself to this tenderness, this happiness.

I trust Jesus so completely that even if I were to see hell open before me and find myself on the brink of the abyss, I should not lose confidence. I should not despair but continue to trust in him.

The most beautiful act of faith
is the one made in darkness,
in sacrifice,
and [with] extreme effort.

51 ❧ WHEN THINGS FALL SHORT

—December 17, 1914 letter to Raffaelina Cerase

You must not be discouraged or let yourself become dejected if your actions have not succeeded as perfectly as you intended. What do you expect? We are made of clay, and not every soil yields the fruits expected by the one who tills it. But let us always humble ourselves and acknowledge that we are nothing if we lack the divine assistance.

To be worried because something we have done has not turned out in accordance with our pure intention shows a lack of humility. This is a clear sign that the person concerned has not entrusted the success of his actions of the divine assistance but has depended too much on his own strength.

52 ❧ TOTAL OFFERING OF OUR WILL IS VERY DIFFICULT

—February 23, 1915 letter to Raffaelina Cerase

God, who has bestowed so many benefits on us, is satisfied with such a very insignificant gift as that of our will. Let us offer it to him in that most sublime prayer, the *Our Father:* Thy Will be done on earth as it is in heaven. Let us offer this will of ours in a total offering and let us do this also in our daily life. Don't let us make our offering like those children who, when they have given something precious as a gift, immediately regret what they have done and begin to cry and ask to have it back.

Total offering of our will is unfortunately very difficult. Our divine Master['s] mind showed him very clearly how difficult it would be, [so he also] asked the Father immediately after he had offered our will to him: Give us this day our daily bread. [Here] I recognize primarily the Eucharist. He was asking leave to remain with us!

53 ❧ The Divine Child

The heavenly Child suffers and cries in the crib so as to make his suffering for us loveable, meritorious, and sought after. He lacked everything so that we learn from him to renounce earthly goods. He was pleased with humble and poor adorers so that we love poverty and prefer the company of the little and simple ones to that of the great of the world.

54 ❧ PEACE

Peace is simplicity of heart, serenity of mind, tranquility of soul, the bond of love. Peace means order, harmony in our whole being; it means continual contentment springing from the knowledge of a good conscience; it is the holy joy of a heart in which God reigns. Peace is the way to perfection, indeed in peace is perfection to be found. The devil, who is well aware of all this, makes every effort to have us lose our peace.

55 ❧ Cry Aloud to God

—February 28, 1915 letter to Raffaelina Cerase

[When your] trial is very hard, I repeat for the umpteenth time that you are not to be afraid, for Jesus is with you even when you see your soul, as it were, on the brink of the precipice. You must invariably lift up your voice to heaven even when desolation invades your soul. Cry aloud along with that most patient man, Job, who when the Lord placed him in the state which you are now experiencing, cried out to him: *Even if you slay me Lord, I will still hope in you.*[1]

---

1. Job 13:15

56 ❧ All Treated Differently, but All Loved

—Undated letter circa 1922-23 to saintly Antonietta Vona[1]

[Among the apostles] there were those who loved and those who were loved. But all, with the exception of the son of perdition, were loved by the divine Master. Not all were treated in the same manner, but according to their needs, characters, and capabilities. Yet all were chosen by the Redeemer.

---

1. See Reading #18, Footnote 2.

57 ❧ An Extremely Pure Divine Light

—*March 26, 1918 letter to Maria Anna Campanile*

Your state of soul is one of desolation or holy spiritual suffering. I assure you that the knowledge of your interior unworthiness is an extremely pure divine light, in which your potentiality to commit any crime, without divine grace, is placed before your consideration. That light is the result of the great mercy of God and was granted to the saints, because it shelters the soul from all feelings of vanity or pride and consolidates humility which is the foundation of true virtue and Christian perfection.

St. Teresa also received this knowledge and says that it is so painful and horrible that it would cause death if the Lord did not sustain the heart.

This knowledge of your potential unworthiness must not be confused with that of true unworthiness. You are mistaking the one for the other. You fear you are … that which is only possible in you.

[Remember that] God can reject everything in a creature conceived in sin, but he absolutely cannot reject the sincere desire to love him.

58 ✦ "A Powerful Battle"

—Written under reluctant obedience to his superiors (Padre Pio speaks of himself in the third person)

This soul had felt strongly from his earliest years the vocation to the religious state, but as he grew older, alas, he began to drink great draughts of this world's vanity. In the heart of this poor creature a powerful battle began between the increasingly strong vocation on the one hand and a sweet but false delight in the things of the world on the other. Perhaps ... the feelings would have triumphed over the spirit and would have smothered the good seed of the divine call. But the Lord who desired this soul for himself was pleased to favor this person with ... [a] vision I ... [will] describe.

While he was meditating one day on his vocation and wondering how he could make up his mind to bid farewell to the world in order to devote himself entirely to God, ... his senses were suddenly suspended and he ... beheld at his side a majestic figure of rare beauty, radiant as the sun. This man took him by the hand and ... [said,] "Come with me, for it is fitting that you fight as a valiant warrior."

59 ⮞ Padre Pio's Painful Farewell to World and Family

—Written by order of his superiors (he speaks of himself in the third person)

It must not be imagined that he had nothing to suffer in the lower [human] part of his soul as he abandoned [to enter the Franciscans] his own family to whom he was strongly attached. He felt even his bones being crushed as this leave-taking approached, and the pain was so intense that he almost fainted.

As the day of his departure drew nearer, this anguish increased. On the last night he spent with his family, the Lord came to console him by yet another vision. He beheld in all their majesty Jesus and his Blessed Mother, who encouraged him and assured him of their predilection. Finally, Jesus placed a hand on his head, and this was sufficient to strengthen the higher part of his soul, so that he shed not a single tear at this painful leave-taking, although at that moment he was suffering agonies in soul and body.

60 ◆ The Saint Stands up for Himself

—September 8, 1911 reply to Padre Benedetto's urging that he return to the friary in spite of a mysterious illness that forced Padre Pio to return to Pietrelcina for several years, since only there could he evade death

How I long to return to the community. The greatest sacrifice I made to the Lord was, in fact, my not being able to live in community. However, I can never believe that you absolutely want me to die. It is true that I have suffered and continue to suffer at home, but I have always been capable of performing my duties [here], something which was never possible when I lived in community. If it were merely a matter of suffering, well and good. But to be a burden and a nuisance to others, without any other result than death, would leave me without an answer.

Moreover, I believe that I too have every duty and right not to deprive myself directly of life at twenty-four years of age. It seems that the Lord wills things this way. Think of me as more dead than alive and then do as you think best, for I am ready to make any sacrifice required by obedience.

61 ❧ How Hard It Is to Believe!

—July 16, 1917 and March 8, 1916 letters to Padre Benedetto

An infinite number of fears assail me at every moment. Temptations against faith which would drive me to deny everything. My dear Father, how hard it is to believe!

*

There are times, moreover, when I am assailed by violent temptations against faith. I am certain that my will does not yield, but my imagination is so inflamed and presents the temptation in such bright colors that sin seems not merely something indifferent but even delightful.

62 ❧ Sin Versus Human Weakness

The devil has only one door through which to enter into our soul: the will. There are no secret doors. There is no sin, if it has not been committed willfully. When the will does not consent, there is no sin but [only] human weakness.

63 ❧ SOMETHING WHICH I CAN NEITHER EXPLAIN NOR UNDERSTAND

—*September 8, 1911 letter to Padre Benedetto*

Yesterday evening something happened to me which I can neither explain nor understand. In the center of the palms of my hands a red patch appeared, about the size of a cent and accompanied by acute pain. The pain was much more acute in the left hand and it still persists. I also feel some pain in the soles of my feet.

This phenomenon has been repeated several times for almost a year now, but for some time past it had not occurred. Do not be disturbed by the fact that this is the first time I have mentioned it, for I was invariably overcome by abominable shame. If you only knew what it costs me to tell you about it now! I have lots of things to tell you but find no words. I can only say that when I am close to Jesus in the Blessed Sacrament, my heart throbs so violently that it seems to me at times that it must burst out of my chest.

Sometimes at the altar my whole body burns in an indescribable manner. My face in particular seems to go on fire. I have no idea, dear Father, what these signs mean.

64 ❧ GOD'S TOUCH

—March 3, 1916 letter to Padre Benedetto

I keep my eyes fixed on the East, in the night which surrounds me, to discover that miraculous star which guided our forebears to the Grotto of Bethlehem. But I strain my eyes in vain to see that luminary rise in the heavens. The more I fix my gaze the dimmer my sight becomes; the greater my effort, the more ardent my search, the deeper the darkness which envelopes me.

Only once did I feel in the deepest recesses of my spirit something so delicate that I do not know how to explain it to you. Without seeing anything, my soul became aware of his presence and then, as I would describe it, he came so close to my soul that I felt his touch. To give you a feeble image of it, it was like what happens when your body feels the pressure of another body against it.

I was seized with the greatest fear, [but] by degrees this fear became a heavenly rapture. It seemed to me that I was no longer in the state of a traveler and I cannot tell you whether or not at that moment I was still aware of being in this body of mine. Only God knows.

65 ✥ Embarrassed and Humiliated by God

—October 22, 1918 letter to Padre Benedetto, following the visible stigmatization he would bear for fifty years

What can I tell you in answer to your questions regarding my crucifixion? My God! What embarrassment and humiliation I suffer by being obliged to explain what you have done to this wretched creature!

On the morning of the twentieth of last month, in the choir, after I had celebrated Mass I yielded to a drowsiness similar to a sweet sleep.[1] All the internal and external senses and even the very faculties of my soul were immersed in indescribable stillness. Absolute silence surrounded and invaded me. I was suddenly filled with great peace and abandonment which effaced everything else and caused a lull in the turmoil. All this … in a flash.

While this was taking place I saw before me a mysterious person similar to the one I had seen on … August 5. The only difference was that his hands and feet and side were dripping blood. This sight terrified me and what I felt … is indescribable. I thought I should die, and really should have died if the Lord had not intervened and

---

1. Padre Benedetto would understand this modest reference to a state of ecstasy.

strengthened my heart which was about to burst out of my chest. The vision disappeared and I became aware that my hands, feet, and side were dripping blood. Imagine the agony I experienced and continue to experience almost every day. The heart wound bleeds continually....

66
A PLEA TO GOD

—October 22, 1918 letter to Padre Benedetto

Dear Father, I am dying of pain because of the wounds and the resulting embarrassment I feel deep in my soul. I am afraid I shall bleed to death if the Lord does not hear my heartfelt supplication to relieve me of this condition. Will Jesus who is so good grant me this grace? Will he at least free me from the embarrassment caused by these outward signs? I will raise my voice and will not stop imploring him until in his mercy he takes away, not the wound or the pain, which is impossible since I wish to be inebriated with pain, but these outward signs which cause me such embarrassment and unbearable humiliation.

67 ∾ Torment That Is Both Lovable and Painful

—November 24, 1918 letter to Padre Benedetto

What a sharp thorn there is in the depths of my soul, which makes me suffer agonies of love day and night! What acute pain I suffer in hands and feet and heart! These are pains which keep me in a continual state of infirmity which, although delightful, is none the less painful and poignant.

In the midst of such torment which is lovable and painful at the same time, two conflicting feelings are present: one which would like to cast off the pain and the other which desires it. The mere thought of having to live for any length of time without this acute yet delightful torment terrifies me, appalls me, and causes me to suffer agonies.

In the midst of this torment I find the strength to utter a painful *fiat*. Oh how sweet and yet how bitter is this "May thy will be done!" It cuts and heals, it wounds and cures, it deals death and at the same times gives life! O sweet torments, why are you so unbearable and so lovable simultaneously[?] O sweet wounds, why is it that although so painful, you apply balm to the soul at the same time?

68 ❧ The Weight and the Bliss of Possessing God

—January 12, 1919 letter to Padre Benedetto

I find it almost impossible to explain the action of the Beloved. He keeps pouring himself completely into the small vase of this creature, and I suffer an unspeakable martyrdom because of my inability to bear the weight of this immense love. How can I carry the Infinite in this little heart of mine? How can I continue to confine him to the narrow cell of my soul? My soul is melting with pain and love, and bitterness and sweetness simultaneously. How can I endure such immense suffering inflicted by the Most High? Because of the exultation of possessing him in me, I cannot refrain from saying with the most holy Virgin: *My spirit rejoices in God my Savior.*[1] Possessing him within me, I am impelled to say with the spouse of the Sacred Song: *I found him whom my soul loves; I held him and would not let him go.*[2] But then when I see myself unable to sustain the weight of this infinite love.... I am filled with terror in case I must leave him because of my incapacity to sustain him in the narrow space of my heart.

---

1. Luke 1:47
2. Song of Songs 3:4

69 ❧ Rejoicing and Sorrow

You must know that I do not have a free moment: a crowd of souls thirsting for Jesus falls upon me so that I don't know which way to turn. Before such an abundant harvest, on [the] one hand I rejoice in the Lord, because I see the ranks of elect souls always increasing and Jesus loved more; and on the other hand I feel broken by such a weight.

*

There have been periods when I [have] heard confessions without interruption for eighteen hours consecutively. I don't have a moment to myself. But God helps me effectively in my ministry. I feel the strength to renounce everything, so long as souls return to Jesus and love Jesus.

70 ❧ Struggling With Human Weakness

—June 14, 1920 letter to Padre Benedetto

My only regret is that, involuntarily and unwittingly, I sometimes raise my voice when correcting people. I realize that this is a shameful weakness, but how can I prevent it if it happens without my being aware of it? Although I pray and groan and complain to Our Lord about it, he has not yet heard me fully. Moreover, in spite of all my watchfulness, I sometimes do what I really detest and want to avoid.

Please continue to recommend me to the divine mercy.

71 ❧ SCOLDING FOR THE LOVE OF GOD

—November 20, 1921 letter to Padre Benedetto

I am consumed by love for God and my neighbor. Please believe me, Father, when I tell you that my occasional outbursts [usually sending individuals out of the confessional without absolution due to feigned or shallow contrition, gestures that resulted in many genuine conversions; see reading #106] are caused precisely by this.

How is it possible to see God saddened by evil and not be saddened likewise? Please believe me, though, when I tell you that at such moments I am by no means shaken or changed in the depths of my soul. I feel nothing except the desire to have and to want what God wants. In him I always feel at rest, at least, internally, while I am sometimes rather uncomfortable [scolding or correcting someone rather harshly] externally.

For my brothers? Alas! How often, not to say always, I have to say to God the Judge, with Moses: *either forgive their sin or else blot me out of the book of life.*[1]

---

1. Exodus 32:31-32

72 ⊸ God's Mission to Padre Pio

—*November 1922 letter to a spiritual daughter*

Infinite praise and thanks be to you, O my God. You hid me away from the eyes of all [in the Capuchin order], but already at that time you had entrusted *a very great mission* to your son. A mission that is known to you and myself alone....

O God! Show yourself more and more to this poor heart of mine, and complete in me the work you have begun. I hear deep within me a voice which says to me repeatedly: sanctify yourself and make others holy.

73 ❧ An Ocean of Sweetness

—*Padre Pio's own account, written under obedience*

I was at the altar for the celebration of Mass. Physical suffering and interior pain competed in torturing my whole poor being....

... As I approached the moment of consuming ... [the Eucharist], I felt myself dying. A mortal sadness pervaded me through and through, and I felt that all was finished for me: my life in time and eternity.

The dominant thought that saddened me ... was of never being able to demonstrate again my reverence and love to divine Goodness. It was not hell so much that terrorized me as the clear knowledge that down there, there is no more love....

I had reached the limit. I had arrived at the culmination of my agony and where I believed I would find death, I found the consolation of life. In the act of consuming the sacred species of the holy Eucharist, a sudden light pervaded me within and I saw clearly the heavenly Mother with the Child Jesus in her arms, who both said to me, "Be calm! We are with you! You belong to us and we are yours."

... That said, I saw no more. Then calm and peace and all my suffering at once disappeared. I felt myself for the whole day drowned in an ocean of sweetness and indescribable love for God and souls.

74 ❧ A Little Flower

—A Memory by Padre Gerardo of Deliceto, who lived with Padre Pio for years

The sixteenth of October was the anniversary of my feast day. As always, I had gone to the office to work. I had not seen the Padre and therefore waited impatiently for 11 o'clock to greet him. That morning I [didn't] hear his rhythmic and dragging footsteps accompanied by loud coughs.

I carried on with my work when, suddenly, it seemed to me that someone had stopped at my door and touched it delicately. Suspicious, I got up and opened the door. It was he, smiling and a bit embarrassed, like a child surprised by his mother while playing some trick.

"Good wishes," he said to me, and gave me a little flower that he had put in the keyhole.

75 ⊷ ONE THING IS NECESSARY

One thing is necessary: to be near Jesus. You know well that at the birth of our Lord the shepherds heard the angelic and divine chants of the heavenly spirits. The Scriptures say so. But they do not say that his Virgin Mother and St. Joseph, who were nearer to the Child, heard the voices of the angels or saw those miracles of splendor. On the contrary, they heard the Child weeping and saw by the light of a poor lantern the eyes of the Divine Child all bathed in tears, in sighs and shivering with cold. Now I ask you: would you not have preferred to be in the dark stable filled with the cries of the little Child, than with the shepherds, beside yourself with joy over those sweet melodies from heaven and the beauties of this wonderful splendor?

76 ❧ ANXIETY

Anxiety is one of the greatest traitors that real virtue and solid devotion can ever have. It would be well to remember that graces and the consolations of prayer are not waters of this earth but of Heaven. Therefore all our efforts are not sufficient to make them fall, even though it be necessary to prepare oneself with great diligence. Instead one must always, humbly and tranquilly, keep one's heart turned to Heaven and wait from there the heavenly dew.

77 ⊸ SOME THOUGHTS ON GRACE AND GLUTTONY

—December 17, 1914 letter to Raffaelina Cerase

Do not sit down to a meal without having prayed first and asked the divine assistance, so that the food you are about to eat for the sustenance of the body may not be harmful to your soul. Picture to yourself the divine Master in your midst with his holy apostles just as he was during the Last Supper before [he]instituted [the Eucharist].

Never rise from the table, moreover, without having given thanks to the Lord. If we act in this way we need have no fear of the wretched sin of gluttony. As you eat, take care not to be too difficult to please in the matter of food, bearing in mind that it is very easy to give in to gluttony. Never eat more than you really need, and endeavor to practice moderation all the time. You should be very ready to refuse what you need rather than [take] what is in excess of your needs. However, I don't mean to say that you should [go] without eating. Let everything be regulated by prudence, which should be the rule in all our actions.

78 ❧ THE HOLY SPIRIT GUIDES HIS PRAYER

—May 19, 1914 letter to Raffaelina Cerase

You complain that I don't answer all your questions and chide me gently on this account. All I can do is ask your pardon and beg you not to be angry with me, for I am not to blame. For some time past I have been suffering from forgetfulness, despite all my good intentions to satisfy every demand made on me. I am told [by my spiritual director] that this is a very special grace of the heavenly Father.

The Lord only allows me to recall those persons and things he wants me to remember. In point of fact, on several occasions our merciful Lord has suggested to me people whom I have never known or even heard of, for the sole purpose of having me present them to him and intercede for them, [whereupon] he never fails to answer my poor feeble prayers. On the other hand, when Jesus doesn't want to answer me, he makes me actually forget to pray for those persons for whom I had firmly decided and intended to pray.

79 ❧ "A HUMAN BEING LIKE EVERYBODY ELSE"

—*Testimony of Andre Mandato of New Jersey*

[When I first started visiting Padre Pio] there wasn't much of a crowd, because it was hard for the people to get there. We could go into the little garden, where there were maybe ten people, and we visited with him. He was jovial, in good humor. He told jokes. When you were by yourself, you would say: "he is a saint." But when he talked with you, you didn't see the saint. You saw a human being like everybody else, smiling, joking. I could touch him. I'd talk with him just [as I'd talk with anyone else].

80 ❧ His "Affable Simplicity"

Padre Pio disarmed everyone with his affable simplicity, even those who had gone on purpose to see the supernatural in him and who wanted to see something [of that extraordinary nature] in him at all costs.

One evening while he was going to the prayer stalls, he said to someone he knew intimately, "Really, I don't feel like praying this evening, and I don't even have the excuse of good intentions, because I really don't want to."

81 ❧ Many Sins Are Forgiven Thee

Have you not for some time loved the Lord? Do you not love him now? Do you not long to love him forever? Therefore: Do not fear! Even conceded that you had committed all the sins in this world, Jesus repeats to you: Many sins are forgiven thee because thou hast loved much!

82 ❧ THREE SUGGESTIONS FOR MAKING SPIRITUAL PROGRESS

—*November 4, 1914 letter to Raffaelina Cerase*

You must take care never to quarrel with anyone, never to contend with anyone. If you act otherwise, it means goodbye to peace and charity. To be inordinately attached to your own opinion is invariably a source and beginning of discord. St. Paul exhorts us to be united in the same mind and the same judgment against this wretched vice.

Be on your guard also against vainglory, a vice to be found in devout persons. It leads us without our being aware of the fact to appear somewhat above others. St. Paul also warns his dear Philippians against this. This great saint, filled with the Spirit of the Lord, saw clearly and fully the evil that would result for those holy Christians if this wretched vice were to succeed in penetrating into their souls. He warned them: *Do nothing from selfishness or conceit.*[1]

Lastly, we must guard against giving priority to what is advantageous to ourselves rather than what benefits others.

---

1. Philippians 2:3

83 ❧ About Distractions

When you have distractions don't distract yourself still more by stopping to consider the *why* and the *wherefore*. Just as a traveler who misses his way, returns to the right road as soon as he is aware of it, you should continue to meditate without stopping in the distractions which you have.

84 ❧ An Incident in Pietrelcina

The young Padre Pio was returning, in the late evening, in the company of the parish priest, Don Salvatore Pannullo, from the Pietrelcina cemetery. When they arrived [at the place] where today stands the Capuchin friary with the adjoining seminary and church, dedicated to the Holy Family, Padre Pio, as if immersed in thought and in prophetic tone, said to the priest: "Don Salvatore, what a beautiful fragrance of incense and sound of angels singing! Can you hear it?" Don Salvatore, surprised, responded: "Piuccio,[1] are you mad or dreaming? There is no smell of incense or sound of angels singing!" Then Padre Pio said: "Father! One day there will rise on this spot a friary and church from where there will ascend to the Lord the incense of prayer and hymns of praise!"

The parish priest, who knew of Pio's holiness, answered: "Well, if it is the will of God."

History proved Padre Pio right.

---

1. An affectionate nickname for Pio.

85 ✎ Delicious Fruits

—March 4, 1915 letter to Raffaelina Cerase

God alone can enlighten the soul with his grace and show that soul what it is. And the more fully a person knows his own wretchedness and unworthiness in God's sight, the more remarkable is the grace that enlightens him and reveals to him what he is.

I understand that the discovery of one's own wretchedness under the action of this divine sun saddens and distresses at the outset. It is a source of pain and of terror for the poor soul that is enlightened in this manner. But console yourself in our most sweet Lord, for when this divine sun will have warmed the earth of your soul with its burning rays, it will cause new plants to spring up, which in due course will yield most delicious fruits, the like of which have never been seen.

Console yourself, then, with this delightful thought, with his beautiful assurance.

86 ❧ Various Thoughts on Prayer

Prayer is the best weapon we have; it is the key to God's heart. You must speak to Jesus not only with your lips but with your heart; in fact on certain occasions you should speak to him only with your heart.

*

One searches for God in books. One finds him in meditation.

*

Pray, hope, and don't worry. Worry is useless. God is merciful and will hear your prayer.

*

All prayers are good when they are accompanied by good intentions and good will.

87 ↔ GOD'S LOVE AND HUMAN INGRATITUDE

—Undated September 1911 letter to Padre Benedetto

When I consider Jesus' love on the one hand and my own ingratitude on the other, my dear Father, I should like to tell him that if I cannot correspond to his love he should stop loving me; only in this way do I feel less guilty. But if Jesus does not love me, what is to become of me? Not to love Jesus and not to be loved any more by him! This is too terrifying a thing for me, and hence it makes me invariably pray Jesus to continue to love me and to help me himself if I do not succeed in loving him as much as he deserves.

88 ❧ THE FIELD OF BATTLE

The field of battle between God and Satan is the human soul. This is where it takes place every moment of our lives. The soul must give free access to our Lord and be completely fortified by him with every kind of weapon. His light must illumine it to fight the darkness of error; he must put on Jesus Christ, his truth and justice, the shield of faith, the word of God to overcome such powerful enemies. To put on Jesus Christ, we must die to ourselves.

89 ❧ There Are Things That Cannot Be Translated Into Human Language

—April 18, 1912 letter to Padre Agostino

Oh how sweet was the colloquy with paradise that morning! It was such that, although I want to tell you all about it, I cannot. There were things which cannot be translated into human language without losing their deep and heavenly meaning. The heart of Jesus and my own—allow me to use the expression—were fused. No longer were two hearts beating but only one. My own heart had disappeared, as a drop of water is lost in the ocean. Jesus was its paradise, its king. My joy was so intense and deep that I could bear no more, and tears of happiness poured down my cheeks.

90 ❧ A First Meeting With Padre Pio

—Written by Maria Gargani, who first met Padre Pio in April 1918

Seeing me appear at the sacristy door (after two years of receiving his spiritual direction by letter), he called me by name and made me enter a little adjoining room where we stopped to talk like two people who had known each other a long time. How sweet the Padre's words were, and what beautiful assurances he gave me concerning my soul! He encouraged me to belong always more to the Lord and to do what I could to let him be glorified in my life!

I felt truly happy, and all the shadows and suffering vanished from my soul. I was silent in his presence, [but] he realized I wanted to tell him many things [so he told me we could meet each afternoon for a while during the fifteen days he would be in town].

I confess that during my conversation with Padre Pio I sipped a great deal of the infusion of the Holy Spirit, which made me enjoy a touch of Tabor, so that the soul desired, like the apostles, to stay there always, in that state of divine elevation of spirit. He taught me, at that time, how to listen to the voice of God.

91 ✧ Holy and Unholy Fears

There is the fear of God and the fear of Judas. Too much fear makes us act without love, and too much confidence [presumption] causes us not to consider and fear the danger that we must overcome. One should help the other, and go together like two sisters. Always, when we become aware of being afraid, of having too much fear, we should remember to become confident. If we are excessively confident, we should become instead a little fearful. Love tends to the object loved; however, in its approach, it is blind. But holy fear enlightens it.

92 ❧ THE CALL OF JESUS

Jesus calls the poor and simple shepherds by means of angels to manifest himself to them. He calls the learned men [the Magi] by means of their science. And all of them, moved interiorly by grace, hasten to adore him.

He calls all of us with divine inspirations and he communicates himself to us with his grace. How many times has he not lovingly invited us also? And with what promptitude have we replied?

My God, I blush and am filled with confusion at having to reply to such a question.

93 ❧ HE READS OTHERS' HEARTS BUT HIS OWN REMAINS A MYSTERY

—March 17, 1916 letter to Padre Agostino

There are so many things that I would like to tell you, Father, but I am unable to do so. I realize that I am a mystery to myself.

94 ❦ "I Started to Believe in Confession"

—Testimony of Andre Mandato of New Jersey

I had been going to church every Sunday but I had no strong belief in Confession. I went very seldom. I started to believe in Confession only after I went to Padre Pio.

The first time I confessed to him, he told *me* what sins I had committed.

95 ❧ PLACE IT ALL IN THE SWEET MERCY OF GOD

—October 18, 1917 letter to Maria Anna Campanile

Don't worry about being unable to remember all your little failings in order to confess them. No, my daughter, you should not afflict yourself for this reason, because as this often happens without your realizing it, in the same way, without your realizing it, you pick yourself up.

The just man doesn't feel or see himself falling seven times a day, but he [still] falls seven times a day. And in the same way, if he falls seven times, then he also picks himself up seven times. Therefore, don't worry about this, but frankly and humbly say [in the confessional] what you remember, and place it in the sweet mercy of God, who places his hand under those who fall without meaning to, so that they might not hurt themselves or be injured. And he lifts them up so quickly that they don't know they have fallen, because the divine hand picked them up when they fell; nor do they know that they have resurrected because they were lifted up so quickly, that they didn't even have time to think about it.

96 ✧ Don't Dwell on Past Misdeeds

In our thoughts and at confession we must not dwell on sins that have been already confessed. Because of our contrition Jesus has forgiven them at the tribunal of penance. There he faced us and our miseries like a creditor in front of a debtor. With a gesture of infinite generosity he tore up and destroyed the bills we signed with our sins, which we could certainly not have paid without the help of his divine clemency. To go back to these sins, to bring them up again just to have them forgiven again, because of doubt that they were really and abundantly remitted, would this not be considered a lack of trust in the goodness which he proved by his tearing up every document of debt contracted through sin?

Dwell on them, if it is a source of comfort for your soul. By all means think of the offenses against justice, wisdom, and the infinite mercy of God, but only for the purpose of weeping redemptive tears of repentance and love.

97 ◦ Two on Temptation

—April 11, 1914 letter to Raffaelina Cerase

I understand that temptations seem to stain rather than purify the soul, but this is not really the case. Let us hear what the saints have to say about it. For you it suffices to know what the great St. Francis de Sales says—namely that temptations are like the soap which when spread on the laundry seems to soil, but in reality cleanses it.

*

—March 2, 1917 letter to Assunta Di Tomaso

You must turn to God when [tempted]; you must hope in him and expect everything that is good from him. Don't voluntarily dwell on what the enemy presents to you. Remember that he who flees wins, and at the first sign of aversion for those [particular] people, you must stop thinking of it and turn to God. Bend your knee before him and with the greatest humility say this short prayer: "Have mercy on me, a poor weakling." Then get up and with holy indifference go about your business.

98 ⊸ THE HOLY FEAR

—January 30 and January 23, 1915 letters to Raffaelina Cerase

You tell me [that] you are afraid of falling into pride. I myself cannot see how a person can become proud on account of the gifts he recognizes in himself. It seems to me that the richer he sees himself to be, the more reason he has to humble himself before the Lord, for the Lord's gifts increase and he can never fully repay the giver of all good things. As for you, what have you in particular to be proud of? What have you that you did not receive? If then you received all, why do you boast as if it were your own?[1]

Whenever the tempter wants you to be puffed up with pride, say to yourself: all that is good in me I have received from God on loan, and I should be a fool to boast of what is not mine.

*

[As for this] fear that you will become proud, don't worry on this account, for this is a holy fear. As long as you are afraid of falling into pride and vainglory you will never be a victim to them. [So] take care that this holy fear never leaves you.

---

1. See 1 Corinthians 4:7

99 ❧ How to Kiss Jesus Without Betraying Him

—September 7, 1915 letter to Raffaelina Cerase

The prophet Isaiah said: *For to us a child is born, to us a son is given.*[1]

This child, Raffaelina, is the affectionate brother, the most loving Spouse of our souls, of whom the sacred spouse of the Song, prefiguring the faithful soul, sought the company and yearned for the divine kisses: *O that you were like a brother to me! If I met you outside, I would kiss you! O that you would kiss me with the kisses of your mouth!*[2] This son is Jesus and we can kiss him without betraying him, give him the kiss and the embrace of grace and love he expects from us and which he promises to return. We can do all this, St. Bernard tells us, by serving him with genuine affection, by carrying out in holy works his heavenly doctrine which we profess by our words.

---

1. Isaiah 9:6
2. Song of Songs 8:1, 1:2

100 ❧ Spiritual Peace in the Storms of Life

—October 10, 1914 letter to Raffaelina Cerase

Remember that spiritual peace can be maintained even in the midst of all the storms of this life. As you know very well, it consists essentially in peaceful relations with those around us, wishing them well in all things. It also consists in being on good terms with God through sanctifying grace. The proof that we are united to God is our moral certainty of not having any mortal sin on our conscience. To sum up, peace consists in having achieved victory over the world, the devil, and our own passions.

This peace which Jesus has brought us can continue quite well to be ours not merely when we enjoy abundant spiritual consolations but when [our hearts are filled] with pain and grief.

101 ⇄ GOODWILL IS SUFFICIENT

—Undated 1917 letter to Christian apostle Assunta Di Tomaso

Live joyfully and courageously, at least in the upper part of the soul, amidst the trials in which the Lord places you. Live joyfully and courageously, I repeat, because the Angel who foretells the birth of our little Savior and Lord announces that he brings tidings of joy, peace, and happiness to men of goodwill. So that there [should be] nobody who does not know that in order to receive this Child it is sufficient to be of goodwill.

102 ◈ FOLLOW BRAVELY IN THE FOOTSTEPS OF THE SAINTS

—September 4, 1916 letter to Maria Gargani

[Don't let] the countless temptations with which you are continually assailed frighten you, because the Holy Spirit forewarns the devout soul who is trying to advance in the ways of the Lord, to prepare itself for temptations.[1]

Therefore, take heart because the sure and infallible sign of the health of a soul is temptation. Let the thought that the lives of the saints were not free from this trial, give us the courage to bear it.

[St. Paul] the apostle of the people, after being taken away to Paradise, was subjected to such a trial that Satan went so far as to hit him.[2] Dear God! Who can read those pages without feeling one's blood freezing? How many tears, how many sighs, how many groans, how many prayers did this holy apostle raise, so that the Lord might withdraw this most painful trial from him! But what was Jesus' reply? Only this: "My grace is sufficient for you."[3] One becomes perfect in weakness.

Therefore take heart. Jesus makes you also hear the same voice he allowed St. Paul to hear. Fight valiantly and you will obtain the reward of strong souls.

---

1. See Sirach 2:1   2. See 2 Corinthians 12:7   3. 2 Corinthians 12:9

103 ✦ An Incident During World War I

During World War I, an old man walked into the friary room, where Padre Pio was absorbed in prayer. He said he was Pietro di Mauro, and that he had died in the friary when it was a home for the elderly on September 18, 1908. He died, he told the young friar, in room number four, having fallen asleep smoking a cigar that set the bed on fire. God, he said, had given him permission to come to Pio and ask his prayers, especially a Mass. Padre Pio, who was still young at the time, found this hard to take. He confided in Padre Paolino of Casacalenda, who had a few doubts of his own.

Padre Paolino had the idea to go down to the town below the friary and check the death records, in which he discovered that this di Mauro, indeed, had died when and how he said. Padre Pio saw the old fellow again, when he had completed his spiritual growth and purification and was on his way to heaven.

104 ❧ Two Places at Once

—*A Bilocation Testimony From Padre Alberto*

One afternoon in May 1928, I saw Padre Pio near the window, staring out, his gaze fixed. He seemed absorbed. I drew near to kiss his hand, but I had the sensation that his hand was stiff. At the same moment, I heard him pronounce the words of absolution in a very clear voice.

Immediately I ran to call Father Tomaso, the superior. The two of us approached Padre Pio, who was pronouncing the last words of absolution. At that Padre Pio gave a jerk as if he had come back out of drowsiness. He turned to us and said: "You're here? I didn't realize you were here."

A few days later a telegram arrived at the friary from a city in northern Italy. The telegram thanked the father superior for having sent Padre Pio to assist a dying man. From the telegram we understood that the man was dying at the exact moment Padre Pio was pronouncing the words of absolution.

105 ❧ The Wife Beater

Giovanni, a taxi driver and Communist, used to get drunk and beat his wife. One night he had done precisely that and then threw himself on the bed. When he hit it he felt somebody shake it violently. He looked towards the end of the bed and, to his amazement, saw a Capuchin friar giving him an icy stare. The friar told him in no uncertain terms what he thought of his behavior and then he seemed to disappear.

Giovanni jumped up from the bed, and [found only his wife in the house]. The poor lady denied all knowledge of any friar, but her husband wouldn't believe her.

The poor woman [who] had prayed at length to Padre Pio [requesting his intercession] had heard of his powers of bilocation. There could be no other explanation for it: Padre Pio had come to help her! [Hearing this,] Giovanni was angry [and] decided to go have "a look" at this friar.

Giovanni [went] to San Giovanni Rotondo. He found Padre Pio, recognized him, and spoke to him. To make a long story short, the convinced Communist, wife beater, and drunk was converted to Christ.

106 ❧ About His Gruffness

—A testimony from Padre Alessio during Padre Pio's last days

One day I was with Padre Pio near the sacristy. It was jam-packed, and we couldn't get through with the wheelchair. I [and another Capuchin were] trying to push our way through the crowd. We were shouting, but the people would not cooperate.

Padre Pio too was shouting: "Let me through!"

Finally when we did get through the crowd, he said: "Don't worry. I didn't get angry in my soul. I was shouting, but my heart was laughing."

The only time some people respected him was when he shouted at them. He told me: "I'll never get angry inside myself. If I ever get angry inside, it won't be for this reason."

The same applies to his roughness in the confessional—it was only to make people live a good life. His harsh words, his shouting, were something that changed people. They would tell me that they had been away from God for forty, fifty, or sixty years. When Padre Pio shouted at them, it was the shock or jolt they needed to come back to God.

107 ◆ Consider Everything a Loan

—May 15, 1915 letter to Raffaelina Cerase

Reflect upon the great humility of the Mother of God, our Mother. The more she was filled with heavenly gifts, the more deeply did she humble herself, so that she was able to say when overshadowed by the Holy Spirit who made her the Mother of God's Son: *Behold the handmaid of the Lord.*[1]

As gifts increase in you, let your humility grow [too], for you must consider that everything is given to you on loan. The increase in gifts must always be combined with humble recognition of such an outstanding benefactor which should burst forth from your heart in the form of continual thanksgiving.

---

1. Luke 1:38

108 ✤ THE SAINT'S LONGING TO BE UNITED TO GOD FOREVER

—September 25, 1915 letter to Padre Agostino

Since the Lord is prolonging my life, I know this is his will. Yet despite the efforts I make, I very seldom succeed in making an act of real resignation, for I always have before my mental gaze the clear knowledge that only by death is true life to be found.

Hence it is that more often than not, unwittingly, I am led to make acts of impatience and utter words of complaint to the most tender Lord to the point of calling him—do not be scandalized, please, Father—of calling him cruel, a tormentor of the souls who desire to love him. But this is not all. When I feel life weighing on me more than ever, when I experience in the depths of my soul something like a most ardent flame which burns without consuming me, then it is that I just cannot bring myself to pronounce a single act of resignation to the divine will in enduring this life.

O God, King of my heart, only Source of all my happiness, how much longer must I wait before I can openly enjoy your ineffable beauty?

109 ❧ His Christmas Joy

—December 28, 1917 letter to Padre Agostino

May the heavenly Child arouse in your heart also all the holy emotions he made me feel during the holy night when he was laid in the poor little crib. Dear God! I cannot describe to you, my dear Father, all that I felt in my heart on that most happy night. My heart seemed to overflow with a holy love for our God become man. The night of the soul continued even at that moment, but I can tell you that in the midst of such pitch [spiritual] darkness, I was surfeited with spiritual joy.

110 ❧ God Looks at Things Very Differently Than We Do

—September 9, 1914 letter to Raffaelina Cerase

You complain that you left Foggia in search of an improvement in your beloved sister's health and unfortunately you did not find it according to your own taste and your own very foolish judgment. The Christian soul looks very differently at God's providence for his creatures. Do you consider a small thing the change which has come about in your sister's soul and also in your own? If you looked at the matter sincerely, you would realize that the order of things has been reversed. You left your hometown in search of better health for your sister, but the divine mercy (see how good God is) willed that you should find chiefly health of soul, to which you paid less attention.

Our God, my dear sister, is admirable in his judgments. You don't understand sufficiently the change which has come about in your sister's soul and in your own, and this is all right.

My way of speaking on this point seems like Greek to you and you find it hard to believe, but the Lord understands what I say.

III ❖ MIRACLE ON A BUS

—Ennio Rossi remembers a day during the summer of 1947

In order to please my wife we went to San Giovanni Rotondo to see Padre Pio. [But] we were told that Padre Pio was ill and that it was impossible to see him. That is how we found ourselves chatting [on a homeward-bound bus] with a distinguished-looking man and a young boy.

The man told us his son had become completely deaf, and the best specialists to whom he had taken him had given no hope of recovery. So he had come to Padre Pio to ask for his powerful intercession with our Lord, and he had been accompanied to Padre Pio's cell, where his son received his blessing with the promise: "Go in peace, I will pray for you."

The young boy was looking out of the window at the countryside. Suddenly he turned to his father and said loudly: "But why are you shouting so?" And surprised to see that we were talking quietly, he immediately realized he was cured and exclaimed delightedly, "Daddy, I can hear! Daddy, I can hear!"

112 ❧ "Do You Doubt It?"

—Testimony from Padre Placido of San Marco in Lamis (a companion of Padre Pio's novitiate days)

Padre Placido was hospitalized with acute liver disease in July 1957. One night via bilocation, Padre Pio appeared at his old friend's bedside, offering comfort and assuring him he would recover. "Be patient," he counseled. A dream? Padre Placido woke much better. He was struck by the mark of a hand on the window by his bed. He was certain this was Padre Pio's hand print. He told everyone who came to his room and soon people were coming to see. The chaplain informed the superior of the local friary who strongly scolded Padre Placido, insisting that this sort of story could do poor Padre Pio no good. But Padre Placido persisted in his belief. Interestingly enough, efforts to clean the window failed. The handprint kept reappearing. Padre Alberto, a confrere, visited and was skeptical. Padre Placido urged he go to San Giovanni Rotondo and question Padre Pio. He did and ended his long query with, "So did you really go there?"

Padre Pio answered, "Do you doubt it?"

Padre Placido got well. And Padre Alberto got a reminder that those who have faith in the "impossible" are not always nuts.

113 ❧ A World War II Testimony

We were at San Giovanni Rotondo from the end of August to the beginning of October 1943, following the bombings [by Allied forces seeking to dislodge the German invaders]. Padre Pio continued his apostolate in the confessional and, when he could, in the parlor, comforting many people.

One afternoon, the Padre, greatly moved, told us that that very morning some people had arrived from Pescara, travelling as best they could [from a city that had been repeatedly bombed all at once from the sea, sky, and land].

[During the bombing] they had fled to the ground floor of a building with five stories and there, terrorized by the continuous explosions, cried and prayed, holding a photograph of Padre Pio and repeating between sobs: "Padre Pio, save us!"

And then came the crucial moment: a bomb crashed through the top floor, then the third, next the second, and finally the first. Imagine the fear and terror of those people when that bomb, making a doomsday din, embedded itself precisely in the ground floor where they had sought refuge!

They cried out in unison invoking the Padre's help: "Padre Pio, save us!"

God answered this plea for the prayer intercession of his saint in a wondrous way: the bomb did not explode.

Hence the grateful delegation coming to thank him for the life-giving prayer of the friar's sacrificial life.

114 ❧ The Case of Agnes Stump

Twenty years old, Agnes had never had even a headache; now after a year of a pain in her left knee, an x-ray diagnosed a tumor, confirmed by a second doctor. [At] Christmas 1967, her father and brother visited Padre Pio, who advised surgery, adding "I will guide the surgeon's hand." On January 2, 1968, surgery was done and healing progressed well until October, a month after Pio's death, when the cancer spread once more. On October 14, 1968, new surgery with tissue biopsied in three institutes revealed "sarcomatosis growth of the mieloplasma tumor." Amputation was advised. A second specialist said amputation wasn't necessary but he advised more surgery to stiffen the leg, which she refused. A third specialist wanted to operate at once.

Agnes visited the tomb of Padre Pio that December 20. Without any of the recommended surgeries but only application of a relic [a blood-stained bandage from the Padre's side wound], Agnes awaited God's help. On April 25, 1969, Padre Pio having come to her shortly before in a beautiful dream, she suddenly began to walk without crutches. Tests showed the disease had stopped spreading. After two years of almost complete immobility, Agnes walked to Padre Pio's tomb in September 1969, kneeling there completely cured.

115 ↔ A HEALING TOUCH

—A testimony from Patricia Gagliano of New Orleans

It was on December 8, 1977, that Father Alessio from Italy was in New Orleans to speak about Padre Pio. I had been suffering very much for ten months with crippling rheumatoid arthritis. My hands were so swollen I could not hold a spoon, and I had terrible pains in my knees and legs. I had been praying to Padre Pio, trusting he would intercede for me in my pain[1] and help me bear my cross.

I approached the table where the relic [of Pio was being displayed] and told Father Alessio that for years I had been praying to Padre Pio for help. Father Alessio said, "Child, why are you suffering?" I said, "I have rheumatoid arthritis in my hands, feet, and knees." Then Father Alessio handed me the relic of Padre Pio to touch my hands with. How long I was privileged to hold the relic I do not remember, but I do remember going home happy. The next morning I awoke and realized my hands were no longer swollen, nor was there pain [in] my knees and legs. I was completely and miraculously cured. Since that morning of December 9, 1977, I have had no sign of pain of swelling in any part of my body. Thanks be to God and the intercession of Padre Pio.

---

1. See 1 Timothy 2:1

116 ❧ HEAVENLY LIGHT

—*October 23, 1914 letter to Raffaelina Cerase*

The finest grace that can be asked on behalf of those who aspire to the spiritual life [is] an increase of heavenly light. This is a light which cannot be acquired either by prolonged study or through human teaching, but which is directly infused by God. When the righteous soul obtains this light, it comes to know and love its God and eternal things in its meditations with extreme clarity and relish. Although it is nothing but a light of faith, it is still sufficient to produce such spiritual consolation that the earth, in the first place, disappears from view, while all that this world can offer is seen to be worthless.

117 ❧ Glory Beyond All Comparison

—August 15, 1914 letter to Raffaelina Cerase

My dear sister, calm the tormenting anxieties of your heart, and banish from your imagination all those distressing thoughts and sentiments. Jesus is always with you, even when you don't feel his presence. He is never so close to you as he is during your spiritual battles. He is always there.

For pity's sake, I beseech you not to wrong him by entertaining the slightest suspicion that he has abandoned you even for a single moment. This is really one of the most diabolical temptations which you must drive far from you as soon as you are aware of it.

Let it be a consolation to know, my dear, that the joys of eternity will be all the more heartfelt and profound, the more numerous the days of humiliation and the years of unhappiness we have known in the present life. This is not just my own opinion. Holy Scripture offers us infallible testimony. [The Psalmist says] *Make us glad as many days as Thou hast afflicted us, and as many years as we have seen evil.*[1] St. Paul the apostle, moreover, [says,] *This slight momentary affliction is preparing us for an eternal weight of glory beyond all comparison.*[2]

---

1. Psalm 90:15
2. 2 Corinthians 4:17

118 ❧ MAKE OUR HEAVENLY FATHER PROUD

—March 30, 1915 letter to Raffaelina Cerase

Live in such a way that the heavenly Father may be proud of you, as he is proud of so many other chosen souls. Live in such a way that you may be able to repeat at every moment with the apostle St. Paul: *Be imitators of me, as I am of Jesus Christ.*[1] Live in such a way, I repeat, that the world will be forced to say of you: "Here is Christ." Oh, for pity's sake, do not consider this an exaggeration! Every Christian who is a true imitator and follower of the fair Nazarene can and must call himself a second Christ and show forth most clearly in his life the entire image of Christ. Oh, if only all Christians were to live up to their vocation, this very land of exile would be changed into a paradise!

---

1. 1 Corinthians 4:16; 11:1

119 ⊷ PADRE PIO'S FIRST PROMISE

"I'll be able to do much more for you when I am in heaven than I can now while I am here on earth," he said before his death on September 23, 1968.

Since then, the holy Capuchin has been seen by a number of people, some of whom—including children—were terminally ill until he came to them as God's messenger of healing. Witnesses include Padre Pio's longtime friend physician Andrea Cardone, who insisted he had seen the dead man "in his mortal flesh." After study by medical experts in the disease, one of the many cures—that of an Italian mother of three—has been singled out for official authentication as a spontaneous healing completely inexplicable by all human explanation, and therefore acceptable as the miracle the Catholic Church requires as "the voice of God" before someone with proven heroic virtue is beatified.

120 ❧ A Sweet Reminder

Padre Pio said: "I belong entirely to everyone. Everyone can say 'Padre Pio is mine.' I deeply love [all humanity]. I love my spiritual children as much as my own soul and even more. I have regenerated them to Jesus through suffering and love. I can forget myself but not my spiritual children. Indeed I can assure you that when the Lord calls me, I will say to him: 'Lord, I will stand at the gates of Heaven until I see all my spiritual children have entered.'"

In 1968 when Padre Pio died, besides leaving a huge hospital called The Home for the Relief of Suffering, *his legacy included 726 prayer groups with 68,000 members. Today the hospital is at full capacity, and there are twenty-two Blessed Pio centers for handicapped children and one center for the blind. Padre Pio's prayer group numbers have doubled or tripled. Six and a half million people visited the Blessed's tomb in 1997. Over seventy thousand crowded together for the 1998 anniversary of his death. In Padre Pio's name, the Capuchin friars of San Giovanni Rotondo are still accepting new prayer groups[1] and new spiritual children[2].*

---

1. To start a new prayer group, write *Prayer Group Centres, 71013 San Giovanni Rotondo (FG), Italy.*
2. To become a spiritual child of Padre Pio, write *Our Lady of Grace Friary, 71013 San Giovanni Rotondo (FG), Italy. Attn. English Office.*

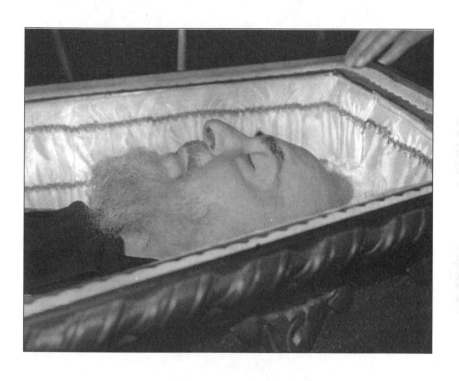

References

1. *Letters Volume IV,* 437–38. (Volume 4 is not yet available in English. The Italian edition, titled *Padre Pio da Pietrelcina, Epistolario IV. Corrispondenza con diverse categorie di persone,* is edited by Melchiorre da Pobladura and Alessandro da Ripabottoni (San Giovanni Rotondo: "Padre Pio da Pietrelcina" Editions, 1984).

2. *Letters Volume III: Correspondence With His Spiritual Daughters (1915–1923),* edited by Melchiorre da Pobladura and Alessandro da Ripabottoni; English version edited by Fr. Alessio Parente (San Giovanni Rotondo: "Padre Pio da Pietrelcina" Editions, 1994), 285.

3. A remark of the Padre's in passing, according to the Padre's spiritual son Father Joseph Pius Martin of Our Lady of Grace Friary, San Giovanni Rotondo, who lived with and assisted him in his later years.

4. *Letters Volume II: Correspondence With the Noblewoman Raffaelina Cerase (1914–1915),* edited by Melchiorre da Pobladura and Alessandro da Ripabottoni, 2nd edition revised and corrected by Father Gerardo Di Flumeri (San Giovanni Rotondo: "Padre Pio da Pietrelcina" Editions, 1987), 425.

5. *Letters II,* 213–14, 423–24.

6. *Letters II,* 99–100.

7. *Letters II,* 399–400.

8. *Letters III,* 669–70.

9. *Letters II,* 401.

10. *Letters II,* 140, 437–38, 461.

11. *Letters III,* 963–64

12. *Letters II,* 152–53, 436.

13. *The Voice of Padre Pio* 28, no. 2 (1998): 13–14.

14. I have condensed P. Bargellini's testimony from *The Voice of Padre Pio* 27, Summer Number (1997): 8–9.

15. *Padre Pio of Pietrelcina: Everybody's Cyrenean* by Alessandro of Ripabottoni, San Giovanni Rotondo, 1987, quoted in *Padre Pio: Our Good Samaritan* by Fr. Alessio Parente, OFM Cap. (San Giovanni Rotondo: "Padre Pio da Pietrelcina" Editions, 1990), 111–12.

16. *Letters II*, 218.

17. *Letters II*, 141–42.

18. *Letters III*, 848–49, 791 and *Letters IV*, 466.

19. *Letters II*, 155–56.

20. *Letters II*, 157–58.

21. *Letters II*, 218, 242.

22. Padre Pio Archives, Capuchin Friary, San Giovanni Rotondo, quoting *Have a Good Day*, edited by Fr. Alessio Parente, 3rd ed. (San Giovanni Rotondo: "Padre Pio da Pietrelcina" Editions, 1995), 154–55.

23. *Letters III*, 730.

24. *Padre Pio: Counsels*, edited by Padre Alessio Parente, (Dublin: Padre Pio Office, 1982), 19.

25. *Per la storia. Padre Pio da Pietrelcina*, by Alberto Del Fante, Bologna, 1950, quoted in *Have a Good Day*, 156.

26. *Letters Volume 1: Correspondence With His Spiritual Directors (1910-1922)*, edited by Melchiorre da Pobladura and Alessandro da Ripabottoni, 3rd edition revised and corrected by Father Gerardo Di Flumeri (San Giovanni Rotondo: "Padre Pio da Pietrelcina" Editions, 1987), 470.

27. *Letters II*, 77.

28. *The Diary of Padre Agostino da San Marco in Lamis*, 35.

29. *Letters I*, 517–18

30. *Letters III*, 971–72.

31. *Letters I*, 519.

32. *Letters II*, 244–45.

33. Comment on Giuseppa is by Padre Pio's American spiritual daughter, Mary

Pyle, who knew his parents well. It can be found in a reminiscence written by Mary in the friary archives. The comments on Grazio are from materials collected by Padre Alessandro of Ripabottoni and Padre Lino Barbati of Prata, reported by C. Bernard Ruffin in *Padre Pio: The True Story* revised and expanded edition (Huntington, Ind.: Our Sunday Visitor, 1991), chapter 2.

34. Fr. Eusebio's statement, taken from what Padre Pio told him, is reported in Padre Alessio Parente's "*Send Me Your Guardian Angel*": *Padre Pio* (Naples: Editions Carlo Tozza, 1984), 19–21.

35. The parish priest's letter is reproduced in "*Send Me Your Guardian Angel*," 32.

36. *Letters II*, 420–21.

37. *Letters II*, 421–22.

38. "*Send Me Your Guardian Angel*," 86–87.

39. *Letters IV*, 965–66 and *Componimenti Scolastici*, edited by Padre Gerardo Di Flumeri, quoted in *Have a Good Day*, 19.

40. *Letters II*, 336–37.

41. *Letters II*, 189, 365.

42. *Padre Pio: Counsels*, 34.

43. *Letters III*, 273.

44. *Padre Pio: Counsels*, 28.

45. *Letters II*, 262.

46. *Letters II*, 504–5.

47. *Letters II*, 308–9 and *Letters III*, 288.

48. *Letters II*, 508.

49. *Letters I*, quoted in *The Voice of Padre Pio* 28, no. 6 (1998): 9.

50. *Consigli-Esortazioni di Padre Pio da Pietrelcina*, Foggia, 1965, 57 quoted in *Have a Good Day*, 105. See also *Letters III*, 665–66.

51. *Letters II*, 290.

52. *Letters II*, 356–58.

53. From a Christmas Meditation written for one of Padre Pio's Spiritual Children.

54. *The Voice of Padre Pio* 28, no. 6 (1998): 13.

55. *Letters II,* 377.

56. *Letters III,* 911.

57. *Letters III,* 957–58.

58. Autobiographical notes, appendix to *Letters I,* 1426–27.

59. Autobiographical notes, appendix to *Letters I,* 1429–30.

60. *Letters I,* 265.

61. *Letters I,* 843, 1014.

62. Padre Pio Archives, Capuchin Friary, San Giovanni Rotondo.

63. *Letters I,* 264–65.

64. *Letters I,* 842.

65. *Letters I,* 1217–18.

66. *Letters I,* 1218.

67. *Letters I,* 1227–28.

68. *Letters I,* 1238–39.

69. *The Voice of Padre Pio* 27, no. 12 (1997): 9, quoting letters to his spiritual directors (no dates given).

70. *Letters I,* 1305.

71. *Letters I,* 1393.

72. *Letters I,* 52.

73. Spiritual diary July–August, 1929. (Although ordered to keep this diary, his eye troubles became so severe that he had to give it up after only a month.)

74. "Padre Pio's Ordinary Side," by Patricia Treece, *The Tidings* Feb. 6, 1998, 19.

75. *Padre Pio: Counsels,* 20.

76. Padre Pio Archives, Capuchin Friary, San Giovanni Rotondo, quoted in *Have a Good Day,* 154–55.

77. *Letters II,* 291–92.

78. *Letters II,* 101–2.

79. *A Padre Pio Profile,* John A. Schug, OFM Cap. (Peterham, Mass.: St. Bede's Publications, 1987), 51.

80. *The Voice of Padre Pio* 27, summer number, (1997): 10.

81. *Padre Pio: Counsels,* 12.

82. *Letters II,* 234–35.

83. *Padre Pio: Counsels,* 23.

84. "Two Prophecies of Padre Pio," by Padre Gerardo, *The Voice of Padre Pio* 28, no. 3 (1998): 10.

85. *Letters II,* 387.

86. *Consigli–Esortazioni de Padre Pio da Pietrelcina,* 39 and 40; *Per la storia: Padre Pio da Pietrelcina,* 547 and 552, all quoted in *Have a Good Day,* 32 and 36.

87. *Letters I,* 267.

88. *Consigli-Esortazioni di Padre Pio da Pietrelcina,* quoted in *Have a Good Day,* 85–86.

89. *Letters I,* 308.

90. *Letters III,* 234.

91. *Per la storia: Padre Pio da Pietrelcina,* quoted in *Have a Good Day,* 27–28.

92. *Letters IV,* 977–78.

93. *Letters I,* 855.

94. *A Padre Pio Profile,* 50.

95. *Letters III,* 953–54.

96. *Tra I misteri della scienza e le luci della fede,* by Giorgio Festa, 1933, quoted in *Have a Good Day,* 69–70.

97. *Letters II,* 75–76 and *Letters III,* 418.

98. *Letters II,* 337, 325.

99. *Letters II,* 506–7.

100. *Letters II,* 202.

101. *Letters III,* 470.

102. *Letters III,* 249–50.

103. Patricia Treece, *Messengers: After-Death Appearances of Saints and Mystics* (Huntington, Ind.: Our Sunday Visitor, 1995), 154–55, reporting an incident found in friary materials.

104. Padre Alberto's testimony can be found in the friary archives.
105. *The Friar of San Giovanni: Tales of Padre Pio* by John McCaffrey, London, 1983, quoted in *Padre Pio: Our Good Samaritan,* 115–16.
106. *A Padre Pio Profile,* 57.
107. *Letters II,* 436–37.
108. *Letters I,* 731.
109. *Letters I,* 1095.
110. *Letters II,* 177.
111. *The Voice of Padre Pio* 28, no. 2 (1998): 11–12.
112. An account in English may be found in *Padre Pio: Our Good Samaritan,* 35–36.
113. Adapted from notes taken down by friar Constantino Capobianco and reported in *The Voice of Padre Pio* 20, no. 4 (1990): 7.
114. Details of Agnes' cure, one of many authenticated healings that have taken place since Padre Pio's death, are in the archives of Our Lady of Grace Friary, San Giovanni Rotondo. A detailed account in English may be found in *Padre Pio: Our Good Samaritan,* 25–30.
115. *The Voice of Padre Pio* 28, no. 3 (1998): 21.
116. *Letters II,* 211.
117. *Letters II,* 168.
118. *Letters II,* 399.
119. Padre Pio Archives, Capuchin Friary, San Giovanni Rotondo.
120. Padre Pio Archives, Capuchin Friary, San Giovanni Rotondo.